Language Activity Book
Student's Edition

ECCE ROMANI

A Latin Reading Program
Second Edition

II-B
Pastimes and Ceremonies

Longman

CHAPTER 43 | AT THE BATHS

Activity 43a

On the three lines to the right of each verb below, write the second, third, and fourth principal parts of the verb. Then on the next set of lines write the requested tense and voice of the verb in the subjunctive, keeping the same person and number as the verb at the left:

	Imperfect Active	Imperfect Passive	Pluperfect Active	Pluperfect Passive
1. dēfricāmus	_____		_____	_____
	_____	_____	_____	_____	_____
2. tergēs	_____		_____	_____
	_____	_____	_____	_____	_____
3. unguitis	_____		_____	_____
	_____	_____	_____	_____	_____
4. custōdiunt	_____		_____	_____
	_____	_____	_____	_____	_____

Activity 43b

Join the first sentence to the second by transforming it into a causal clause introduced by *cum* and having its verb in the subjunctive. Then translate the new sentence. The first set is done for you.

1. Cornēlius sē nimis exercuerat.
Cornēlius maximē dēfessus erat.

Cum Cornēlius sē nimis exercuisset, maximē dēfessus erat. _____

Since Cornelius had exercised too much, he was very tired. _____

2. Cornēlius in caldāriō vapōrem vix patī poterat.
Cornēlius haud multum ibi morātus est.

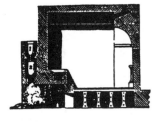

_____

_____

_____

3. Cornēlius vapōre caldāriī paene oppressus erat.
Cornēlius in tepidārium regressus est.

_____

_____

_____

4. Cornēlius tergērī volēbat.
Cornēlius ē tepidāriō ēgressus est.

_____

_____

5. Virī in thermīs diū collocūtī erant.
Virī domum sērō discessērunt.

_____

_____

Activity 43c

Join the first sentence to the second by transforming it into a circumstantial clause introduced by *cum* and having its verb in the subjunctive. Then translate the new sentence. The first set is done for you.

1. Cornēlius in Campum Mārtium dēscenderat.
   Cornēlius in Thermās Nerōnēās ingressus est.

   Cum Cornēlius in Campum Mārtium dēscendisset, in Thermās Nerōnēās ingressus est.

   When Cornelius had descended into the Campus Martius, he entered the Baths of Nero.

2. Cornēlius amīcīs heri occurrerat.
   Cornēlius amīcōs dē rēbus urbānīs rogāvit.

   _____

   _____

3. Cornēlius in vestibulum ingrediēbātur.
   Cornēlius ab amīcīs salūtābātur.

   _____

   _____

4. Cornēlius ab amīcīs salūtātus erat.
   Cornēlius in apodytērium iniit.

   _____

   _____

5. Cornēlius et amīcī in palaestram inībant.
   Multī cīvēs ibi sē exercēbant.

   _____

   _____

   _____

6. Aliī lūctābantur.
   Cornēlius cum duōbus amīcīs trigōne lūdēbat.

   _____

   _____

Activity 43d

Transform the following questions into indirect questions after the verb *rogābant* and translate the resulting sentence. The first set is done for you.

1. Quid audīvistī dē rēbus urbānīs, Tite?

   Rogābant *Titum quid dē rēbus urbānīs audīvisset.*

   They were asking Titus what he had heard about the affairs of the city.

2. Quid agitur in senātū, Tite?

   Rogābant _____

   _____

3. Quid prīnceps contrā incendia facit, Tite?

   Rogābant _____

   _____

4. Quī hominēs praeclārī iam in urbe adsunt, Tite?

   Rogābant _____

   _____

5. Cūr paene collāpsus es in caldāriō, Cornēlī?

   Rogābant _____

   _____

6. Cūr ē thermīs nunc ēgrederis, Cornēlī?

   Rogābant _____

   _____

Activity 43e

Translate into Latin:

1. A bald old man clothed in a red tunic, after paying his fee, went into the entrance passage of the Palatine Baths.

   _____

2. Having entered the exercise ground he began to play ball with two long-haired boys.

   _____

3. He was refusing to pick up balls that had fallen to the ground. (Use **nōlō.**)

   _____

4. Since a slave standing nearby was giving him other balls, the old man was able to play for a long time.

   _____

5. After a drink of wine, the old man, exhausted, fell to the ground.

   _____

6. Never has so ridiculous a thing been seen!

   _____

Activity 43f
Give one English word derived from each of the following Latin words:

1. calor: _____

2. (dē)fricō: _____

3. digitus: _____

4. repetō: _____

5. senex: _____

6. unguō: _____

7. vestibulum: _____

8. vestīmenta: _____

Activity 43g
With the aid of an English dictionary, give the Latin word from which each of the following English words is ultimately derived:

1. dishevelled: _____

2. fool: _____

3. anoint: _____

What language influenced these words on their route from Latin into English?

_____

Activity 44a

Combine the following sentences by reducing the first to a perfect participle and inserting it into the second. Include any other words from the first sentence needed to make sense. Then translate the new sentence into English. The first set is done for you.

1. Coquus vocātus est.
Coquus ab omnibus laudātus est.

Coquus vocātus ab omnibus laudātus est.
_____

The cook was summoned and praised by all.
_____

2. Puerī ē lūdō ēgressī sunt.
Puerī ad thermās vēnērunt.

_____

_____

3. Puerī vestīmenta exuērunt.
Puerī vestīmenta servīs trādunt.

_____

_____

4. Fūrēs vestīmenta surripuērunt.
Fūrēs vestīmenta in urbe vēndunt.

_____

_____

5. Vestīmenta surrepta sunt.
Sextus fūrem cum vestīmentīs currentem vīdit.

_____

_____

6. Fūr captus est.
Dominus īrā commōtus fūrī appropinquāvit.

_____

_____

7. Fūr captus est.
Dominus ā fūre vestīmenta surrepta ēripuit.

_____

_____

8. Fūr captus est.
Dominus in fronte fūris litterās FUR inussit.

_____

_____

9. Sextus ā dominō laudātus est.
  Cornēlius Sextō praemium dat.

  _____

  _____

10. Trēs fūrēs captī sunt.
  Frontēs trium fūrum litterās inustās exhibent.

  _____

  _____

praemium, -ī, n., _reward_   **exhibeō, -ēre, -uī, -itus,** to _show,_ _display_

inūrō, inūrere, inussī, inustus, to _brand_

Activity 44b

Fill in the blanks with present active participles of the verbs in parentheses. Make the participle agree with the underlined noun or nouns. Be sure to use the correct endings (gender, case, and number). Then translate the sentence into English.

1. <u>Marcus et Sextus</u> ē lūdō _____ domum īre in animō habuērunt. (ēgredī)

  _____

2. <u>Puerī</u> verba Eucleidis _____ maximē gaudēbant. (audīre)

  _____

3. Via ad thermās ferēns erat plēna <u>puerōrum</u> _____ ē lūdō. (venīre)

  _____

4. <u>Puerōs</u> in thermās _____ amīcī salūtāvērunt. (intrāre)

  _____

5. <u>Puerīs</u> vestīmenta _____ Eucleidēs, "Nunc in palaestram exeāmus," inquit. (exuere)

  _____

  _____

6. <u>Servō</u> vestīmenta _____ nōmen erat Asellus. (custōdīre)

  _____

7. Magnus est numerus <u>fūrum</u> vestīmenta _____ in hāc urbe. (surripere)

  _____

8. Eucleidēs <u>servō</u> vestīmenta dīligenter _____ praemium dedit. (custōdīre)

  _____

9. Vestīmenta ā <u>servō</u> _____ surrepta sunt. (dormīre)

  _____

10. <u>Fūrem</u> ex apodytēriō _____ Sextus cōnspexit. (ēgredī)

  _____

Activity 44c
Combine the following sentences by transforming the first into an ablative absolute.
Translate the new sentence. The first set is done for you.

1. Puerī verba Eucleidis audīvērunt.
   Puerī maximē gaudēbant.
   Verbīs Eucleidis audītīs, puerī maximē gaudēbant.

   The boys were very happy when they heard Eucleides' words.

2. Puerī in apodytērium ingrediēbantur.
   Fūr sē subitō cēlāvit.

3. Puerī vestīmenta exuērunt.
   Puerī in tepidārium intrāvērunt.

4. Puerī in tepidārium intrābant.
   Fūr vestīmenta surripuit.

5. Sextus aeger erat.
   Puerī ē tepidāriō ēgressī sunt.

6. Vestīmenta surrepta sunt.
   Sextus īrātus fīēbat.

7. Fūr aufugiēbat.
   Sextus magnā vōce clāmābat.

8. Sextus clāmābat.
   Fūr lāpsus in aquam cecidit.

9. Fūr captus est.
   Dominus Sextō praemium dedit.

10. Litterae in fronte inussae sunt.
    Fūr trīstis erat.

Activity 44d

Many English words are derived from *prehendō, prehendere, prehendī, prehēnsus*, often incorporating prefixes. Give definitions of the following derivatives of this verb. Use an English dictionary. Note in each case how the meaning of the English word is related to that of the Latin verb and the prefix:

1. apprehend: _____

2. apprehensive: _____

3. apprentice: _____

   _____

4. apprise: _____

5. comprehend: _____

6. comprise: _____

7. emprise: _____

8. enterprise: _____

9. entrepreneur: _____

10. impregnable: _____

11. impresario: _____

    _____

12. misapprehension: _____

13. prehensile: _____

14. prison: _____

15. reprehend: _____

16. reprehensible: _____

17. reprisal: _____

18. surprise: _____

    _____

CHAPTER 45 | PYRAMUS AND THISBE

Activity 45a

The following are extracts from the story of Pyramus and Thisbe as told by the Roman poet Ovid. The meter is dactylic hexameter. Write translations of the extracts on a separate sheet or sheets of paper. You may use the vocabulary at the end of Book II-B or Book II in addition to the vocabulary and aids that àre given with each Latin passage.

Pȳramus et Thisbē, iuvenum pulcherrimus alter,
altera, quās Oriēns habuit, praelāta puellīs,
contiguās tenuēre domōs, ubi dīcitur altam
coctilibus mūrīs cīnxisse Semīramis urbem.

> **Oriēns, Orientis,** m., *the eastern part of the world, the orient*
> **praelātus, -a, -um** + dat., *preferred to, excelling*
> **contiguus, -a, -um,** *neighboring, adjoining*
> **tenuēre = tenuērunt**
> **coctilis, -is, -e,** *made of sun-baked bricks*
> **cingō, cingere, cīnxī, cīnctus,** *to surround*
> **Semīramis, Semīramidis,** f., *Semiramis (a legendary ninth century B.C. queen of Assyria, who was said to have built the city of Babylon)*

Thisbe, having gone out to the woods to meet Pyramus, sees a lioness.

Quam procul ad lūnae radiōs Babylōnia Thisbē   5
vīdit et obscūrum timidō pede fūgit in antrum,
dumque fugit, tergō vēlāmina lāpsa relīquit.

> **quam:** i.e., *the lioness* (**leaena, -ae**)
> **radius, -ī,** m., *ray, beam*
> **obscūrus, -a, -um,** *dark*
> **antrum, -ī,** n., *cave*

A short time later Pyramus comes into the woods and finds the veil that the lioness had seen and torn with its bloody mouth.

Pȳramus ut vērō vestem quoque sanguine tīnctam
repperit, "Ūna duōs," inquit, "nox perdet amantēs,
ē quibus illa fuit longā dignissima vītā;   10
nostra nocēns anima est. Ego tē, miseranda, perēmī,
in loca plēna metūs quī iussī nocte venīrēs
nec prior hūc vēnī."

> **tīnctus, -a, -um,** *wet, stained*
> **reperiō, reperīre, repperī, repertus,** *to find*
> **dignus, -a, -um** + abl., *worthy of*
> **nostra = mea**
> **nocēns, nocentis,** *guilty*
> **miserandus, -a, -um,** *pitiable*
> **perimō, perimere, perēmī, perēmptus,** *to destroy*
> **venīrēs:** *(that) you should come*

After Pyramus stabs himself, Thisbe comes out of hiding and finds the body of her lover.

"Pȳrame," clāmāvit, "quis tē mihi cāsus adēmit?
Pȳrame, respondē! Tua tē cārissima Thisbē   15
nōminat; exaudī vultūsque attolle iacentēs!"
Ad nōmen Thisbēs oculōs ā morte gravātōs
Pȳramus ērēxit vīsāque recondidit illā.

> **quis:** interrogative adjective, modifying **cāsus**
> **cāsus, -ūs,** m., *accident, misfortune*
> **adimō, adimere, adēmī, adēmptus** + dat., *to take away from*
> **exaudiō, exaudīre, exaudīvī, exaudītus,** *to listen*
> **attollō, attollere,** *to lift up*
> **gravātus, -a, -um,** *weighted down*
> **ērigō, ērigere, ērēxī, ērēctus,** *to lift up, raise*
> **recondō, recondere, recondidī, reconditus,** *to put away; to close (the eyes) again*

Upon realizing what had happened, Thisbe decided to die with her lover.

"Persequar extīnctum lētīque miserrima dīcar
causa comesque tuī: quīque ā mē morte revellī   20
(heu!) sōlā poterās, poteris nec morte revellī."

> **persequor, persequī, persecūtus sum,** *to follow*
> **extīnctus, -a, -um,** *dead* (supply **tē** with **extīnctum**)
> **lētum, -ī,** n., *death*
> **comes, comitis,** m./f., *companion*
> **revellō, revellere, revellī, revulsus,** *to tear away, remove*
> **heu!** *alas!*

Before killing herself, Thisbe prayed on behalf of Pyramus and herself that they would be buried in the same tomb and that the fruit of the mulberry tree under which they died would henceforth be funereal black rather than its former white.

Vōta tamen tetigēre deōs, tetigēre parentēs;
nam color in pōmō est, ubi permātūruit, āter,
quodque rogīs superest, ūnā requiēscit in urnā.

> **vōtum, -ī,** n., *prayer*
> **tangō, tangere, tetigī, tāctus,** *to touch* (**tetigēre = tetigērunt**)
> **pōmum, -ī,** n., *fruit*
> **permātūrēscō, permātūrēscere, permātūruī,** *to ripen fully*
> **āter, ātra, ātrum,** *black*
> **supersum, superesse, superfuī,** *to be left over, remain*
> **requiēscō, requiēscere, requiēvī, requiētūrus,** *to rest*
> **urna, -ae,** f., *funerary urn*

NOUNS

1st Declension

balneae, -ārum, f. pl., *baths*

lacrima, -ae, f., *tear*

palaestra, -ae, f., *exercise ground*

rīma, -ae, f., *crack*

sella, -ae, f., *sedan chair, seat, chair*

spēlunca, -ae, f., *cave*

thermae, -ārum, f. pl., *public baths*

Thermae Nerōnēae, -ārum, f. pl., *the Baths of Nero*

Thisbē, Thisbēs, f., *Thisbe*

2nd Declension

apodytērium, -ī, n., *changing-room*

caldārium, -ī, n., *hot room (at baths)*

Campus Mārtius, -ī, m., *the Plain of Mars on the outskirts of Rome*

cōnsilium, -ī, n., *plan*

    cōnsilium capere, *to adopt a plan*

digitus, -ī, m., *finger*

frīgidārium, -ī, n., *cold room (at baths)*

harpastum, -ī, n., *heavy hand ball*

linteum, -ī, n., *towel*

ōsculum, -ī, n., *kiss*

pālus, -ī, m., *post*

pavīmentum, -ī, n., *tiled floor*

Pȳramus, -ī, m., *Pyramus*

tepidārium, -ī, n., *warm room (at baths)*

trigōn, trigōnis, m., *ball game involving three people, ball (used in this game)*

unguentum, -ī, n., *ointment, perfume, oil*

vestibulum, -ī, n., *entrance passage*

3rd Declension

Babylōn, Babylōnis, f., *Babylon*

calor, calōris, m., *heat*

follis, follis, gen. pl., **follium,** m., *bag*

fūr, fūris, m., *thief*

leō, leōnis, m., *lion*

senex, senis, m., *old man*

strigilis, strigilis, gen. pl., **strigilium,** f., *strigil, scraper*

vapor, vapōris, m., *steam*

vēlāmen, vēlāminis, n., *veil, shawl*

virgō, virginis, f., *maiden*

4th Declension

vultus, -ūs, m., *face, expression*

ADJECTIVES

1st and 2nd Declension

calvus, -a, -um, *bald*

capillātus, -a, -um, *with long hair*

indūtus, -a, -um, *clothed*

īnscius, -a, -um, *not knowing*

Nerōnēus, -a, -um, *of Nero*

rīdiculus, -a, -um, *absurd, laughable*

sanguineus, -a, -um, *bloodstained*

uterque, utraque, utrumque, *each (of two), both*

varius, -a, -um, *different, various, varied*

3rd Declension

commūnis, -is, -e, *common*

prior, prior, prius, gen., **priōris,** *first (of two), previous*

VERBS

1st Conjugation

concrepō, concrepāre, concrepuī, *to snap (the fingers)*

dēfricō, dēfricāre, dēfricuī, dēfrictus, *to rub down*

2nd Conjugation

exerceō, -ēre, -uī, -itus, *to exercise, train*

tergeō, tergēre, tersī, tersus, *to dry, wipe*

3rd Conjugation

aspergō, aspergere, aspersī, aspersus, *to sprinkle, splash, spatter*

    ōre sanguine aspersō, *his mouth spattered with blood*

cognōscō, cognōscere, cognōvī, cognitus, *to find out, learn*

exprimō, exprimere, expressī, expressus, *to press out, express*

occīdō, occīdere, occīdī, occīsus, *to kill*

perdō, perdere, perdidī, perditus, *to destroy*

prehendō, prehendere, prehendī, prehēnsus, *to seize*

repetō, repetere, repetīvī, repetītus, *to pick up, recover*

unguō, unguere, ūnxī, ūnctus, *to anoint, smear with oil*

valedīcō, valedīcere, valedīxī, valedictūrus, *to say goodbye*

3rd Conjugation -iō

cōnfugiō, cōnfugere, cōnfūgī, *to flee for refuge*

surripiō, surripere, surripuī, surreptus, *to steal*

4th Conjugation

conveniō, convenīre, convēnī, conventūrus, *to come together, meet, assemble*

exsiliō, exsilīre, exsiluī, *to leap out*

sentiō, sentīre, sēnsī, sēnsus, *to feel, notice*

DEPONENT VERBS

1st Conjugation

lūctor, lūctārī, lūctātus sum, *to wrestle*

rixor, -ārī, -ātus sum, *to quarrel*

2nd Conjugation

polliceor, pollicērī, pollicitus sum, *to promise*

3rd Conjugation

lābor, lābī, lāpsus sum, *to slip, fall*

subsequor, subsequī, subsecūtus sum, *to follow (up)*

3rd Conjugation -iō

prōgredior, prōgredī, prōgressus sum, *to go forward, advance*

4th Conjugation

orior, orīrī, ortus sum, *to rise*

PREPOSITION

contrā + acc., *against*

ADVERBS

haud, *not*
prope, *near, nearby*
quō, *there, to that place*
sēcrētō, *secretly*

CONJUNCTION

nec, *and . . . not*

MISCELLANEOUS

exeāmus, *let us go out*
mē custōde, *with me on guard, while I am on guard*
noctū, *at night*
pecūniā datā, *with his money having been given, after paying his entrance fee*
quibus verbīs audītīs, *with which words having been heard, when they had heard this*
vīnō sūmptō, *with wine having been taken, after a drink of wine*

Activity Xa

Translate into Latin, using the story in Exercise Xf of *Pastimes and Ceremonies* as a guide:

1. Arachne, since she was the most skilled of all, was famous for her art. (Use a **cum** causal clause.)

   _____

2. Since Arachne was weaving very beautiful fabrics, many curious people used to come to her cottage. (Use an ablative absolute.)

   _____

3. Even the nymphs, intending to visit Arachne, left behind woods, mountains, waves. (Use a future active participle.)

   _____

4. All asked who had taught Arachne.

   _____

5. Minerva, when she had heard the girl replying arrogantly, came to her cottage.

   _____

6. Having entered the cottage, she warned Arachne.

   _____

7. While Arachne was wondering why Minerva herself had not come, the goddess said, "I have come!" (Use a **cum** circumstantial clause.)

   _____

8. When the goddess's pretended form was put aside, Arachne proposed a contest. (Use an ablative absolute.)

   _____

9. Minerva, since she had not been able to defeat Arachne in the contest, was very angry. (Use a **cum** causal clause.)

   _____

10. Arachne, when her head had been reduced in size, became a spider. (Use a **cum** circumstantial clause.)

   _____

Activity Xb

Find and circle the Latin words for the English words listed to the right. Words may go in a horizontal, vertical, or diagonal direction, but they are never backward.

```
n  u  h  e  d  s  p  e  l  u  n  c  a  o  r
h  a  u  d  m  u  l  t  o  p  o  s  t  m  v
l  s  m  b  f  m  y  i  e  a  f  x  u  c  l
c  r  p  l  e  t  a  p  x  o  u  i  f  q  n
s  c  a  l  d  a  r  i  u  m  r  o  r  u  v
b  d  v  o  r  e  s  u  i  e  e  y  i  r  i
i  m  i  i  p  e  t  a  t  h  s  i  g  d  n
u  o  m  o  r  o  z  y  i  m  l  o  i  h  o
m  d  e  n  u  m  d  h  o  o  r  h  d  p  s
s  e  n  e  x  o  e  x  d  r  i  u  a  m  u
f  x  t  e  p  i  d  a  r  i  u  m  r  u  m
l  o  a  a  r  t  s  i  o  t  m  i  i  h  p
c  r  r  m  e  x  e  a  m  u  s  h  u  o  t
e  f  s  t  h  s  a  e  h  r  i  u  m  t  o
p  t  l  p  e  c  u  n  i  a  d  a  t  a  s
```

1. on the ground
2. let us go out
3. not much later
4. thieves *(nom.)*
5. after a drink of wine
6. warm room
7. by chance
8. cave
9. cold room
10. intending to die
11. after paying his entrance fee
12. hot room
13. old man
14. changing room
15. tiled floors

Activity Xc

Fill in the spaces at the right with translations of the English at the left. When you are finished, copy the circled letters in order and you will discover a Latin *sententia*. Write its meaning in the space provided.

1. on hearing these words 〇 __ __ __ __ __   __ __ __ __ __ __
   __ 〇 __ __ __ __ __

2. about to fear __ __ __ 〇 __ __ __ __ __

3. while I am on guard __ __   __ __ __ __ __ 〇 __

4. to try *(imperf. subjunctive, 3rd pl.)* __ __ __ __ 〇 __ __ __ __ __

5. (having been) sent *(masc. nom. pl.)* __ __ __ __ 〇

6. praising __ __ __ 〇 __ __ __

7. you *(sing.)* will climb __ __ __ __ __ __ 〇 __

8. to be *(imperf. subjunctive, 1st pl.)* __ __ __ __ __ __ __ 〇

9. with a thief __ __ 〇 __ 〇 __ __

10. face __ __ __ 〇 __ __

11. about to throw *(fem. abl. sing.)* __ __ __ __ __ __ __ 〇

12. but __ 〇

13. his mouth spattered with blood 〇 __ __   __ __ __ __ __ __ __ 〇 __
    __ __ __ __ __ __ 〇

14. kiss *(noun)* __ __ __ __ __ __ 〇

15 not knowing __ __ __ __ 〇 __ __

16. rising __ __ __ __ 〇 __

17. to that place, there 〇 __

18. I am sorry 〇 __ __ __ __

19. to send *(imperf. subjunctive, 1st pl.)* __ __ __ __ __ __ O __ __ __

20. when you had been called *(abl. absolute)* O O __ __ __ __ __ __

21. bag O __ __ __ __ __

22. veil, shawl __ __ __ O __ __ __ __

23. away from the city __ O O __ __ __

24. to slip O __ __ __

25. loving *(masc./fem. nom. sing.)* O __ __ O __

26. to try *(use deponent verb)* __ __ __ O O __

27. around __ __ O __ O

28. having been moved *(masc. nom. sing.)* __ __ O __ __

29. each (of two) *(neut. nom. sing.)* O __ __ __ __ __ __ __

30. girl, maiden __ __ O __ __

Copy circled letters here: __ __ __   __ __ __ __ __?   __ __ __ __ __ __

__ __ __ __ __ __   __ __   __ __   __ __ __ __ __

__ __ __ __ __ __ __ __.

Meaning of **sententia:** _____

CHAPTER 46 A RAINY DAY

Activity 46a
Keeping to the story in Chapter 46, answer the following questions with complete Latin sentences.

1. What was Marcus intending to do today? _____

   _____

2. Why didn't he do what he wanted? (Give two reasons.) _____

   _____

3. How long were the boys playing "bandits"? _____

   _____

4. Why did the boys begin shouting? _____

   _____

5. Why did Cornelia enter the atrium?_____

   _____

6. Why is Cornelia going to give the doll to Davus' daughter? _____

   _____

7. Did Sextus obey Cornelius? What did Sextus do?_____

   _____

Activity 46b
Study this example:

> Dāvus est īrācundus.
> Quid dīcis?
> Dīcō Dāvum esse īrācundum.

Following the above pattern, combine these sentences:

1. Sextus est puer temerārius.
   Quid dīcis?

   Dīcō _____

2. Pater Marcī est crūdēlis.
   Quid putat Sextus?

   Sextus putat_____

3. Cornēlius est senātor Rōmānus.
   Quid dīcitis?

   Dīcimus _____

4. Adstantēs fūrem ex aquā extrahunt.
   Quid vidēs?

   Videō adstantēs_____

(continued)

5. Puer exclāmat, "Calōrem patī nōn possum."

   Quid exclāmat puer?

   Puer exclāmat sē _____

6. Cornēlius īrātus ad puerōs venit.

   Quid puerī vident?

   Puerī vident_____

7. Sextus pūpam abripit.

   Quid Eucleidēs videt?

   Eucleidēs videt _____

8. Cornēlia pūpā lūdit.

   Quid Sextus crēdit?

   Sextus crēdit _____

9. Puerī molestissimī fīunt.

   Quid Eucleidēs sentit?

   Eucleidēs sentit _____

10. Puerī digitīs micant et magnā vōce clāmant.

    Quid Flāvia et Cornēlia audiunt?

    Flāvia et Cornēlia audiunt _____

Activity 46c

Fill in the blanks with Latin words to match the English cues:

1. _____ad Campum Mārtium dēscendere vīs, ubi pluit? (Surely . . . not?)

2. _____vīs digitīs micāre? (Don't . . . ?)

3. "_____ _____ _____, puerī!" inquit
   Eucleidēs. "Crās nōn pluet." ("Cheer up!")

4. Ubi pluit, puerī ē_____currunt. (courtyard)

5. _____Cornēlius vēnit et Sextum _____Cornēliae reddere
   iussit. (Finally) (the doll)

6. Sextus _____ _____. (obeyed Cornelius)

7. _____ _____latrunculīs lūdēbant. (Both boys)

8. Iam hōra _____sexta erat, ubi Titus ad Thermās Nerōnēās dēscendit.
   (almost)

9. "Quid _____ _____fīliae Dāvī?" rogat Cornēlia, nam

   _____ _____eius est. (will I give as a gift) (birthday)

10. _____līberīs _____, ubi pater īrātus erit? (What will
    happen to)

Activity 46d

Translate into Latin:

1. What is happening to Canus?

_____

2. The emperor ordered him to be killed, but they say that he is not worried.

_____

3. Everyone knows that even with his guards he is quietly playing chess and counting his pawns.

_____

4. The guards believe that Canus is winning, even when advancing to his death.

_____

       pawn, **calculus, -ī,** m.

Activity 46e

Fill in the blanks in the following statements. You will have to use both an English and a Latin dictionary in this activity. Give Latin verbs in their infinitive form.

1. The English word *collide* comes from the Latin prefix **con-**, meaning_____, and the Latin verb _____, meaning _____. The Latin diphthong *ae* becomes _____when the simple verb is compounded with the prefix. The Latin verb **collīdere** means to_____. To collide is to_____.

2. The English word *delude* comes from the Latin prefix **dē-**, meaning_____ _____, and the Latin verb _____, meaning _____. The Latin verb **dēlūdere** means to_____. To delude is to_____.

3. The English word *illusion* comes from the Latin prefix **in-**, meaning_____, and the Latin verb _____. The Latin verb **illūdere** means _____. An illusion is _____.

4. The English word *dispute* comes from the Latin prefix **dis-**, meaning_____, and the Latin verb _____, meaning _____. The Latin verb **disputāre** means to_____. To dispute is to_____.

5. The English word *impute* comes from the Latin prefix **in-**, meaning _____, and the Latin verb_____. The Latin verb **imputāre** means to_____ _____. To impute is to_____.

CHAPTER 47

LOOKING FORWARD TO THE GAMES

Activity 47a

Using story 47 as a guide, write the Latin for:

1. Titus knows that Cornelius is always busy. _____

   _____

2. Titus is sure that Cornelius will not work tomorrow. _____

   _____

3. Titus hopes that Cornelius will go to the games tomorrow. _____

   _____

4. He does not realize that his brother said this as a joke. _____

   _____

5. Everyone knows that slaves finished the amphitheater. _____

   _____

6. I see that the streets are full of people. _____

   _____

7. Cornelius thinks that Aurelia will not go to the games. _____

   _____

8. It is agreed that Aurelia does not like blood. _____

   _____

9. Titus replies that he will go to the amphitheater at dawn. _____

   _____

10. I hope that we will see you in the amphitheater. _____

    _____

Activity 47b

Complete the following. The first set is done for you.

1. Titus dīcit sē ad Thermās Nerōnēās heri _descendisse_ .

   Titus dīcit sē ad Thermās Nerōnēās hodiē <u>dēscendere</u>.

   Titus dīcit sē ad Thermās Nerōnēās crās _dēscēnsūrum esse_ .

2. Titus dīcit cīvēs sē heri <u>ūnxisse</u> et <u>dēfricuisse</u>.

   hodiē _____ et _dēfricāre_ .

   crās _____ et _____ .

3. Amīcī Titī sciunt eum omnia heri _____ .

   hodiē _____ .

   crās <u>cognitūrum esse</u>.

4. Crēdimus senem calvum pilās heri nōn _____.

                hodiē nōn <u>repetere</u>.

                crās nōn _____.

5. Crēdimus fūrēs vestīmenta heri _____.

                hodiē <u>surripere</u>.

                crās _____.

6. Scīmus nōs fūrēs heri <u>prehendisse</u>.

                hodiē _____.

                crās _____.

7. Cōnstat fūrēs in palaestram heri _____.

                hodiē <u>cōnfugere</u>.

8. Crēdimus Thisbēn Pȳramō amōrem heri _____.

                hodiē <u>exprimere</u>.

                crās _____.

9. Cōnstat amantēs invītōs heri <u>valedīxisse</u>.

                hodiē _____.

                crās _____.

10. Dīcunt bovem sanguine leōnem heri _____.

                hodiē <u>aspergere</u>.

                crās _____.

11. Pȳramus crēdit sē Thisbēn heri _____.

                hodiē _____.

                crās <u>occīsūrum esse</u>.

12. Cōnstat Thisbēn sine Pȳramō vīvere hodiē <u>nōlle</u>.

                heri _____.

13 Thisbē crēdit vēlāmen suum Pȳramum heri <u>perdidisse</u>.

                hodiē _____.

                crās _____.

Activity 47c
Supply appropriate forms of the irregular verb *mālō*:

1. CORNĒLIUS: Vīsne ad mūnera crās īre, Aurēlia?

2. AURĒLIA: Ego domī manēre _____.

3. CORNĒLIUS: _____-ne, Marce, ad mūnera īre an domī manēre?

4. AURĒLIA: Marcus certē ad mūnera īre _____ quam domī manēre.

5. MARCUS: Ego et Titus ad mūnera īre _____ quam domī manēre.

6. AURĒLIA: _____-ne, Cornēlia et Sexte, ad mūnera īre an domī manēre?

7. CORNĒLIUS: Cornēlia et Sextus ad mūnera īre _____, sed domī manēbunt.

    an, conj., *or*

Activity 47d

Translate the following into Latin:

1. It is agreed that Vespasian and Titus built an amphitheater and baths in place of Nero's Domus Aurea.

   _____

   _____

2. They say that the Roman people admire the warm baths and that many men will come from every part of the empire to the games.

   _____

   _____

3. They say that Titus has given Rome back to itself.

   _____

in place of, **in locō** + gen. *to admire,* **admīror, -ārī, -ātus sum** *empire,* **imperium, -ī,** n.

Activity 47e

1. **Using a Latin dictionary, find meanings for the following:**

   ōtium _____

   ōtiōsus _____

   ōtiōsē _____

   ōtior _____

2. **Using an English dictionary, find the meaning of the following:**

   otiose _____

3. **Using a Latin dictionary, find meanings for the following:**

   negōtium _____

   negōtiōsus _____

   negōtiātiō _____

   negōtiātor _____

   negōtior _____

4. **Explain the relationship between the words *ōtium* and *negōtium*.**

   _____

   _____

5. **Give meanings for the following English words (use a dictionary as necessary):**

   negotiate _____

   negotiation _____

   negotiator _____

   negotiable _____

   negotiant _____

6. **Using a Latin dictionary, find three meanings for the following:**

   mūnus   **a.** _____   **b.** _____   **c.** _____

7. **Explain briefly what each of the following English words means and how it is related to the Latin word *mūnus*. (Use an English dictionary as necessary.)**

common _____

_____

immune _____

_____

municipal _____

_____

munificence _____

_____

remuneration _____

_____

8. **Using a Latin dictionary, find five different meanings for the following:**

cōnstāre   a. _____

            b. _____

            c. _____

            d. _____

            e. _____

9. **Using a Latin dictionary, find five different meanings for the following:**

mātūrus   a. _____

            b. _____

            c. _____

            d. _____

            e. _____

10. **Explain briefly what each of the following English words means and how it is related to the Latin word *mātūrus*. (Use an English dictionary as necessary.)**

immature _____

_____

mature _____

_____

premature _____

_____

A DAY AT THE COLOSSEUM

Activity 48a

Keeping to the first story in Chapter 48, answer the following questions with complete Latin sentences:

1. Quid Marcus et Cornēlius in viīs prope amphitheātrum vīdērunt et audīvērunt?

   _____

   _____

2. Quid fēcerant multī extrā amphitheātrī portās? _____

   _____

3. Quid fēcit Cornēlius cum amphitheātrum intrāret? _____

   _____

4. Cūr Marcus attonitus erat? _____

   _____

5. Quem Marcus vīdit? _____

6. Quid dē Titō Marcus sciēbat? _____

   _____

7. Quis intrāvit cum silentium factum esset? _____

   _____

8. Ubi gladiātōrēs cōnstitērunt? _____

   _____

9. Quī post gladiātōrēs intrāvērunt? _____

   _____

10. Quam diū et quōmodo gladiātōrum paria pugnābant? _____

    _____

11. Quō ante merīdiem Marcō et Cornēliō redeundum erat? _____

    _____

12. Volēbatne Cornēlius Marcum merīdiānōs hodiē vidēre? _____

    _____

13. Cūr Titus manēre mālēbat? _____

    _____

Activity 48b

Fill in the blanks with Latin words to match the English cues:

1. _____ Marcus _____ hominēs nōn vīderat. (Previously) (so many)

2. In amphitheātrō Marcus et Cornēlius _____ et subitō vīdērunt Titum iam cōnsēdisse. (looked around)

3. Locus in amphitheātrō _____ erat _____.
   (for women: dat. pl.) (reserved)

4. Erat alter locus _____. (for the senators)

5. Gladiātōrēs sē _____, _____, et oculōs

   _____ ad _____. (turned) (stopped) (raised)
   (the imperial seat of honor)

6. _____ _____ et _____.
   (The fighting went on) (fiercely) (bravely)

7. Marcus erat _____. (astounded)

8. Marcus _____ _____ gladiātōrēs _____

   _____ spectābat. (seized with amazement) (join battle)

9. Marcus _____ quot gladiātōrēs pugnārent. (was trying to guess)

10. Marcus _____ _____ _____ vidēbit.
    (the frenzy) (of the midday fighters) (at another time)

11. Spectātōrēs Caesarem, amōrem ac _____ generis hūmānī,

    _____. (delight) (pointed out)

12. Cum gladiātōrēs _____ pulvīnar cōnstitissent, magnopere _____.
    (opposite) (there was shouting)

Activity 48c

Translate the following into English, paying particular attention to the tenses of the infinitives:

1. Marcus dīcit patrem epistulam cōnfēcisse.

   _____

2. Marcus dīxit patrem epistulam cōnfēcisse.

   _____

3. Marcus dīxit patrem epistulam crās cōnfectūrum esse.

   _____

4. Marcus dīxit epistulam ā patre cōnfectam esse.

   _____

5. Marcus dīcit epistulam ā patre cōnficī.

   _____

6. Marcus dīxit epistulam ā patre cōnficī.

   _____

(continued)

7. Videō Cornēlium ad Cūriam festīnāre.

_____

8. Audīvī Cornēlium ad Cūriam festīnāvisse.

_____

9. Audīvī Cornēlium ad Cūriam festīnātūrum esse.

_____

10. Audīvī praedōnēs Eucleidem secūtōs esse.

_____

11. Putāvī praedōnēs Eucleidem secūtūrōs esse.

_____

12. Vīdī Eucleidem praedōnēs magnopere verērī.

_____

13. Scīvī praedōnēs Eucleidem numquam veritūrōs esse.

_____

14. Audīvī prīncipem saepe ā gladiātōribus salūtātum esse.

_____

15. Marcus spērābat patrem sē ad amphitheātrum iterum ductūrum esse.

_____

Activity 48d

Translate into English and into Latin:

1. a. Cum Titus ad Thermās Nerōnēās pervēnisset, pecūniam custōdī dedit.

    _____

   b. When everyone had entered the hot room, a thief stole our clothes.

    _____

2. a. Nesciēbāmus quis vestīmenta nostra surripuisset.

    _____

   b. We did not know where (**quō**) the thief had fled.

    _____

3. a. Fūre in aquam lāpsō, vestīmenta nostra arripuimus.

    _____

   b. When the thief had been seized, we put on our clothes.

    _____

4. a. Nōn crēdō Cornēliam pūpā lūdere.

    _____

   b. I know that she will give the doll to Davus' daughter.

    _____

5. a. Crēdēbam Cornēliam ōlim pūpīs lūsisse.

    _____

   b. I thought that Cornelia would give the doll to Davus' daughter tomorrow.

    _____

Activity 48e

The words in each of the following sets are related to one another in meaning. You have already met at least one word in each set. Try to deduce the meaning of the other words. Use a Latin dictionary when you are uncertain of the exact meaning of a word. Write appropriate definitions below each word:

Noun	*Verb*	*Adjective*	*Adverb*
1. lībertus	līberō	līber	līberāliter
_____	_____	_____	_____
lībertās		līberālis	
_____		_____	
līberātor			
_____			
2. amor	amō	amābilis	amābiliter
_____	_____	_____	_____
amātor			
_____			
amīcitia			
_____			
amīca			
_____			
inimīcus			
_____			
3. timor	timeō	timidus	timidē
_____	_____	_____	_____
4. fortitūdō		fortis	fortiter
_____		_____	_____
5. laus	laudō	laudābilis	laudābiliter
_____	_____	_____	_____
			_____
laudātor			
_____			
6. calor	caleō	calidus	calidē
_____	_____	_____	_____

(continued)

Noun	Verb	Adjective	Adverb
7. crūdēlitās		crūdēlis	crudēliter
_____		_____	_____
8. magnitūdō		magnus	magnopere
_____		_____	_____
			magis
			_____
			maximē
			_____
9. imperium	imperō	imperātōrius	imperābiliter
_____	_____	_____	_____
		_____	
imperātor			
_____			
10. cupīdō	cupiō	cupidus	cupidē
_____	_____	_____	_____
cupiditās			
_____			
11. mīrātor	mīror	mīrus	mīrē
_____	_____	_____	_____
	_____		
		mīrābilis	
		_____	
admīrātiō	admīror		
_____	_____		

Activity 49a

The following is the complete story of Androcles (or Androclus, as spelled here) and the lion as told by Aulus Gellius, a Roman scholar and writer of the second half of the second century A.D. Read the sections that are given in English translation and write your own translations of the sections that are given in Latin. Write your translations on a separate sheet or sheets of paper. You may use the vocabulary at the end of *Pastimes and Ceremonies* in addition to the vocabulary and aids that are given with each Latin passage.

Apion, who was called Plistonices, was a man who had read widely and possessed an extensive and varied knowledge of things Greek. In his works, which are quite famous, is contained an account of almost all the remarkable things that are to be seen and heard in Egypt. Now, in his accounts of what he claims to have heard or read he is perhaps too wordy and wrongly tries to show off—for he is always advertising his own learning. But, this incident that he describes in the fifth book of his *Egyptian History*, he declares that he neither heard nor read but saw himself with his own eyes in the city of Rome.

"In Circō Maximō," inquit, "vēnātiōnis amplissimae pugna populō dabātur. Eius reī, Rōmae cum forte essem, spectātor," inquit, "fuī. Multae ibi saevientēs ferae, magnitūdinēs bēstiārum excellentēs omniumque invīsitāta aut fōrma erat aut ferōcia. Sed praeter alia omnia leōnum," inquit, "immānitās admīrātiōnī fuit praeterque omnēs cēterōs ūnus."

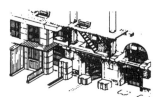

amplissimus, -a, -um, *very large, very impressive*
saeviēns, saevientis, *raging, savage*
fera, -ae, f., *wild animal* (supply the verb **erant** with **ferae**)
magnitūdō, magnitūdinis, f., *size* (translate the pl. as sing.)
excellō, excellere, *to surpass* (the participle modifies **ferae**)
invīsitātus, -a, -um, *never seen before, unusual*
fōrma, -ae, f., *appearance, shape*
ferōcia, -ae, f. (deduce from **ferōx**)
immānitās, immānitātis, f., (deduce from **immānis**; translate the gen. pl. **leōnum** with **immānitās**)

"This one lion had attracted the attention and eyes of all because of the activity and huge size of his body, his terrific and deep roar, the development of his muscles, and the mane streaming over his shoulders."

"Intrōductus erat inter complūrēs cēterōs ad pugnam bēstiārum datōs servus virī cōnsulāris; eī servō Androclus nōmen fuit. Hunc ille leō ubi vīdit procul, repente," inquit, "quasi admīrāns stetit ac deinde sēnsim atque placidē, tamquam noscitābundus, ad hominem accēdit."

cōnsulāris, -is, -e, *of consular rank*   **noscitābundus, -a, -um,** *recognizing*
repente, adv., *suddenly*   **accēdō, accēdere, accessī, accessus,** *to approach*
sēnsim, adv., *gradually*

"Then, wagging his tail in a mild and caressing way, after the manner and fashion of fawning dogs, he came close to the man, who was now half dead with fright, and gently licked his feet and hands. The man Androclus, while submitting to the caresses of so fierce a beast, regained his lost courage and gradually turned his eyes to look at the lion."

"Tum quasi mūtuā recognitiōne factā laetōs," inquit, "et grātulābundōs vidērēs hominem et leōnem."

grātulābundus, -a, -um, *offering congratulations*

(continued)

Apion says that at this sight, so truly astonishing, the people broke out into great shouts; and Gaius Caesar called Androclus to him and asked why that fiercest of lions had spared him alone. Then Androclus related a strange and surprising story. "My master," he said, "was governing Africa with proconsular authority. While there, I was forced by his undeserved and daily whippings to run away. Hoping to find hiding places safe from my master, the ruler of that country, I took refuge in lonely plains and deserts, intending, if food should fail me, to seek death in some form."

"Tum sōle mediō," inquit, "rabidō et flagrantī specum quandam nactus remōtam latebrōsamque, in eam mē penetrō et recondō. Neque multō post ad eandem specum vēnit hic leō, dēbilī ūnō et cruentō pede, gemitūs ēdēns et murmura, dolōrem cruciātumque vulneris commiserantia."

> **rabidus, -a, -um,** *raging, fierce*
> **flagrāns, flagrantis,** *blazing, scorching* (three adjectives modify **sōle**)
> **specus, -ūs,** f., *cave* (note the gender)
> **nancīscor, nancīscī, nactus sum,** *to get, find, arrive at*
> **latebrōsus, -a, -um,** *offering a place to hide*
> **penetrō, -āre, -āvī, -ātus,** *to cause to go into a thing or place*
>   **mē penetrō,** *I enter*
> **recondō, recondere, recondidī, reconditus,** *to put away, hide*
> **dēbilis, -is, -e,** *feeble, lame* (note the ablative absolute)
> **cruentus, -a, -um,** *bloody*
> **gemitus, -ūs,** m. (deduce from **gemō**)
> **ēdō, ēdere, ēdidī, ēditus,** *to give forth*
> **cruciātus, -ūs,** m., *torture, pain*
> **commiseror, -ārī, -ātus sum,** *to seek pity/sympathy for something* (the "something" will
>   be an object in the accusative case; the participle **commiserantia** modifies **gemitūs . . .**
>   **et murmura**)

And then, at the first sight of the approaching lion, Androclus said that his mind was overwhelmed with fear and dread. "But when the lion," he said, "had entered what was evidently his own lair and saw me cowering at a distance, he approached me mildly and gently, and lifting up his foot, was clearly showing it to me and holding it out as if to ask for help."

"Ibi," inquit, "ego stirpem ingentem, vēstīgiō pedis eius haerentem, revellī conceptamque saniem vulnere intimō expressī accūrātiusque sine magnā iam formīdine siccāvī penitus atque dētersī cruōrem. Illā tunc meā operā et medellā levātus, pede in manibus meīs positō, recubuit et quiēvit atque ex eō diē triennium tōtum ego et leō in eādem specū eōdemque et vīctū vīximus."

> **vēstīgiō:** abl. of place where with **haerentem**
> **revellō, revellere, revellī, revulsus,** *to pull out*
> **conceptus, -a, -um,** *that has been produced*
> **saniēs, -ēī,** f., *discharge from a wound, pus*
> **intimus, -a, -um,** *the inmost part of* (**volnere intimō** is abl. of place where, to be taken with
>   **conceptum**)
> **accūrātius,** comparative of **accūrātē,** adv., *carefully*
> **formīdō, formīdinis,** f., *fear*
> **siccō, -āre, -āvī, -ātus,** *to dry*
> **penitus,** adv., *from within, thoroughly*

dētergeō, dētergēre, dētersī, dētersus, *to wipe off,* *clean away*
cruor, cruōris, m., *blood*
tunc, adv., *then*
opera, -ae, f., *effort*
medella, -ae, f., *treatment, cure*
levō, -āre, -āvī, -ātus, *to raise up, relieve,* *make well*
triennium, -ī, n., *a period of three years*
vīctus, -ūs, m., *food*

"For he used to bring for me to the cave the choicest parts of the game that he took in hunting. Having no means of making a fire, I dried the meat in the noonday sun and ate it. But," he said, "after I had finally grown tired of that wild life, I left the cave when the lion had gone off to hunt, and after traveling nearly three days, I was seen and caught by some soldiers and taken from Africa to Rome to my master. He at once had me condemned to death by being thrown to the wild beasts. But," he said, "I see that this lion was also captured, after I left him, and that he is now repaying me for my kindness and for my curing him."

Apion records that Androclus told this story, and that when it had been made known to the people by being written out in full on a tablet and carried around the Circus, at the request of all Androclus was freed, acquitted, and presented with the lion by vote of the people.

"Posteā," inquit, "vidēbāmus Androclum et leōnem, lōrō tenuī revīnctum, urbe tōtā circum tabernās īre, dōnārī aere Androclum, flōribus spargī leōnem, omnēs ubīque obviōs dīcere: 'Hic est leo hospes hominis, hic est homō medicus leōnis.'"

lōrum, -ī, n., *leather thong*
tenuis, -is, -e, *thin*
revinciō, revincīre, revīnxī, revīnctus, *to tie, bind*
taberna, -ae, f., *shop*
aes, aeris, n., *bronze, money*
flōs, flōris, m., *flower*
spargō, spargere, sparsī, sparsus, *to scatter, sprinkle*
ubīque, adv., *everywhere*
obvius, -a, -um, *who comes in the way/meets*

Activity 49b

Answer the following questions in brief paragraphs in English on a separate sheet of paper:

1. How credible is Apion as a storyteller? How credible is his story?

2. When Androclus first addresses Caesar, how does he seek to gain sympathy for himself?

3. What human traits does the lion exhibit?

4. How do both Androclus and the lion display sympathy for one another and generosity during their encounter and life in the cave?

5. Why does Androclus' master condemn him to death?

6. What character trait does Androclus' master lack that both the lion and Androclus possess?

7. What is the moral of the story?

Activity 49c

Just as Seneca in the 1st century A.D. protested at the brutality of the gladiatorial combats (see "Opposition to the Games," Chapter 49), so Cicero had protested in the 1st century B.C. The following is from a letter written by Cicero in 55 B.C. to his friend M. Marius. Cicero is telling Marius what he has seen in recent days, including wild-beast hunts in the arena.

With the help of the translation provided, read the following Latin passages. Then answer in English the questions below on a separate sheet or sheets of paper.

Reliquae sunt vēnātiōnēs bīnae per diēs quīnque; magnificae, nēmō negat. Sed quae potest hominī esse polītō dēlectātiō, cum aut homō imbecillus ā valentissimā bēstiā laniātur, aut praeclāra bēstia vēnābulō trānsverberātur? Quae tamen, sī videnda sunt, saepe vīdistī; neque nōs, quī haec spectāvimus, quidquam novī vīdimus.

Extrēmus elephantōrum diēs fuit; in quō admīrātiō magna vulgī atque turbae, dēlectātiō nūlla exstitit. Quīn etiam misericordia quaedam cōnsecūta est atque opīniō eiusmodi, esse quandam illī bēluae cum genere hūmānō societātem.

There remain the wild-beast hunts, two a day for five days—magnificent; there is no denying it. But what pleasure can it possibly be to a man of culture, when either a puny human being is mangled by a most powerful beast, or a splendid beast is transfixed with a hunting-spear? And even if all this is something to be seen, you have seen it more than once; and I, who was a spectator, saw nothing new in it.

The last day was that of the elephants, and on that day the mob and crowd were greatly impressed, but manifested no pleasure. Indeed, the result was a certain compassion and a kind of feeling that that huge beast has a fellowship with the human race.

1. Why is it that the wild-beast hunts that are described as **magnificae** give no pleasure to the cultured man (**hominī...polītō**)?

2. Cicero mentions that some of the spectators were greatly impressed with the elephants. Do you think that Cicero was impressed with them? How does Cicero refer to the people who were impressed?

3. Why did the people pity the elephants?

4. Compare Cicero's reaction to the wild-beast hunt with Seneca's to the midday exhibition in the arena ("Opposition to the Games," Chapter 49). How are their reactions similar? How different?

NOUNS

1st Declension

arēna, -ae, f., *sand, arena*
bēstia, -ae, f., *beast*
cavea, -ae, f., *cage*
dēliciae, -ārum, f. pl., *delight*
dīvitiae, -ārum, f. pl., *wealth, riches*
hasta, -ae, f., *spear*
lanista, -ae, m., *trainer*
lūdia, -ae, f., *female slave attached to a gladiatorial school*
pugna, -ae, f., *fight, battle*
    pugnam committere, *to join battle*
pūpa, -ae, f., *doll*
tessera, -ae, f., *ticket*
turba, -ae, f., *crowd, mob; cause of confusion/turmoil*

2nd Declension

bēstiārius, -ī, m., *a person who fights wild beasts in the arena*
dōnum, -ī, n., *gift*
    dōnō (dat.) **dare**, *to give as a gift*
latrunculus, -ī, m., *robber*; pl., *pawns (a game like chess)*
    lūdus latrunculōrum, *game of bandits*
locārius, -ī, m., *scalper*
lūdus, -ī, m., *school, game*
merīdiānī, -ōrum, m. pl., *midday fighters*
peristȳlium, -ī, n., *peristyle (courtyard surrounded with a colonnade)*
populus, -ī, m., *people*
saeculum, -ī, n., *age, era*
supposītīcius, -ī, m., *substitute*
tālī, -ōrum, m. pl., *knucklebones*

3rd Declension

admīrātiō, admīrātiōnis, f., *amazement*
    admīrātiōnī esse, *to be a source of amazement*
Androclēs, Androclis or **Androclus, -ī**, m., *Androcles*
appāritor, appāritōris, m., *public servant, gate-keeper*
cassis, cassidis, f., *plumed metal helmet*
cornicen, cornicinis, m., *horn-player*
crūdēlitās, crūdēlitātis, f., *cruelty*
epigramma, epigrammatis, n., *epigram*
furor, furōris, m., *frenzy*
gladiātor, gladiātōris, m., *gladiator*
imperātor, imperātōris, m., *commander, emperor*
Mārtiālis, Marcus Valerius, m., *Martial (poet, ca. A.D. 40–104)*
mīlia, mīlium, n. pl., *thousands*
mūnus, mūneris, n., *gladiatorial show*; pl., *games*
paria, parium, n. pl., *pairs*
pulvīnar, pulvīnāris, n., *imperial seat (at games)*
recognitiō, recognitiōnis, f., *recognition*
stirps, stirpis, gen. pl., **stirpium**, f., *thorn*
tigris, tigris, gen. pl., **tigrium**, m./f., *tiger*
tremor, tremōris, m., *cause of fright, terror*
tridēns, tridentis, gen. pl., **tridentium**, m., *trident*
tubicen, tubicinis, m., *trumpet-player*
voluptās, voluptātis, f., *pleasure, delight*

4th Declension

cōnsēnsus, -ūs, m., *agreement*
impetus, -ūs, m., *attack*

5th Declension

diēs nātālis, diēī, nātālis, m., *birthday*
merīdiēs, ēī, m., *noon, midday*

ADJECTIVES

1st and 2nd Declension

aequoreus, -a, -um, *belonging to the sea*
belliger, belligera, belligerum, *warlike*
bēstiārius, -a, -um, *involving wild beasts*
claudus, -a, -um, *lame*
exanimātus, -a, -um, *paralyzed*
hūmānus, -a, -um, *human*
languidus, -a, -um, *drooping*
mānsuētus, -a, -um, *tame*
Mārtius, -a, -um, *connected with Mars (the god of war and combat)*
mūtuus, -a, -um, *mutual*
negōtiōsus, -a, -um, *busy*
obstupefactus, -a, -um, *astounded*
superbus, -a, -um, *proud, arrogant*
timendus, -a, -um, *to be feared*
ūniversus, -a, -um, *the whole of, entire*

3rd Declension

immānis, -is, -e, *huge*
memorābilis, -is, -e, *memorable*
mināx, minācis, *menacing*
mīrābilis, -is, -e, *wonderful*
mītis, -is, -e, *gentle*
nātālis, -is, -e, *of/belonging to birth*

Indeclinable

tot, *so many*

VERBS

1st Conjugation

condemnō, -āre, -āvī, -ātus, *to condemn*
cōnstat, *it is agreed*
iugulō, -āre, -āvī, -ātus, *to kill, murder*
    Iugulā! *Murder him!*
līberō, -āre, -āvī, -ātus, *to set free*
micō, micāre, micuī, *to move quickly to and from, flash*
    digitīs micāre, *to play* morra
putō, -āre, -āvī, -ātus, *to think, consider*
reservō, -āre, -āvī, -ātus, *to reserve*
spērō, -āre, -āvī, -ātus, *to hope*

2nd Conjugation

contineō, continēre, continuī, contentus, *to confine, hold*
doleō, -ēre, -uī, -itūrus, *to be sorry, be sad, be in pain*
lateō, -ēre, -uī, *to lie in hiding, hide*

3rd Conjugation

cōgō, cōgere, coēgī, coāctus, *to compel, force*
committō, committere, commīsī, commissus, *to bring together, entrust*

cōnsistō, cōnsistere, cōnstitī, *to halt, stop, stand*

convertō, convertere, convertī, conversus, *to turn (around)*

ēdūcō, ēdūcere, ēdūxī, ēductus, *to lead out*

immittō, immittere, immīsī, immissus, *to send in, release*

incēdō, incēdere, incessī, *to go in, march in*

intellegō, intellegere, intellēxī, intellēctus, *to understand, realize*

intrōdūcō, intrōdūcere, intrōdūxī, intrōductus, *to bring in*

laedō, laedere, laesī, laesus, *to harm*

lambō, lambere, lambī, *to lick*

ostendō, ostendere, ostendī, ostentus, *to show, point out*

parcō, parcere, pepercī + dat., *to spare*

3rd Conjugation -iō

abripiō, abripere, abripuī, abreptus, *to snatch away*

circumspiciō, circumspicere, circumspexī, circumspectus, *to look around*

coniciō, conicere, coniēcī, coniectus, *to throw, throw together; to figure out, guess*

incipiō, incipere, incēpī, inceptus, *to begin*

4th Conjugation

feriō, -īre, -īvī, -ītus, *to hit, strike, kill*

Irregular

fīō, fierī, factus sum, *to become, be made, happen*

mālō, mālle, māluī, *to prefer*

referō, referre, retullī, relātus, *to bring back, report, write down*

tollō, tollere, sustulī, sublātus, *to lift, raise*

DEPONENT VERBS

1st Conjugation

admīror, -ārī, -ātus sum, *to wonder (at)*

mīror, -ārī, -ātus sum, *to wonder*

3rd Conjugation

vēscor, vēscī + abl., *to feed (on)*

3rd Conjugation -iō

congredior, congredī, congressus sum, *to come together*

PREPOSITION

contrā + acc., *against, opposite, in front of, facing*

ADVERBS

ācriter, *fiercely*

aliās, *at another time*

blandē, *in a coaxing/winning manner*

clēmenter, *in a kindly manner*

ferē, *almost, approximately*

mātūrē, *early*

placidē, *gently, peacefully, quietly, tamely*

postrēmō, *finally*

quasi, *as if*

rē vērā, *really, actually*

ter, *three times*

INTERROGATIVE WORD

Num . . . ? *Surely . . . not . . . ? (introduces a question that expects the answer "no")*

MISCELLANEOUS

ambō, ambae, ambō, *both*

clāmātum est, *there was shouting*

crēdidissem, *I would have believed*

epistula est cōnficienda, *the letter must be finished*

Hoc habet! *He's hit!*

Mitte! *Let him go!*

nōbīs redeundum est, *we must return*

pār impār, *odds or evens (a game)*

prō certō habēre, *to be certain*

pugnābātur, *the fighting went on*

Quid Sextō fiet? *What will happen to Sextus?*

quō maior . . . , eō plūs . . . , *the greater . . . , the more . . .*

redeāmus, *let us return*

Verberā! *Thrash him!*

Activity XIa

Translate into Latin, using the story in Exercise XIg of *Pastimes and Ceremonies* as a guide:

1. Appius Julius in his letter says that it is difficult to write about Jerusalem besieged by Titus.

   _____

2. His grandson wanted to know what had happened.

   _____

3. The grandson knows that the governor of Judaea was expelled.

   _____

4. The Jews knew that the Romans would return, but they preferred to defend their freedom.

   _____

5. The Romans heard that the Jews were divided into three factions.

   _____

6. It is agreed that many Jews were killed before the Romans returned.

   _____

7. We know that Vespasian sent his son with four legions.

   _____

8. The Jews were soon about to lack food.

   _____

9. We know that the citadel was destroyed by Titus, the temple burned.

   _____

10. Titus, who did not understand the character of the Jews, thought that they would soon hand over their arms.

    _____

Activity XIb

Find and circle the Latin words for the English words listed below. Words may go in a horizontal, vertical, or diagonal direction, but they are never backward.

```
a  l  p  a  n  e  m  e  t  c  i  r  c  e  n  s  e  s  t  p
v  m  a  u  l  i  o  l  p  v  o  c  a  l  e  s  r  c  u  c
e  v  p  r  u  a  n  l  r  e  v  e  r  a  e  y  p  u  s  p
c  i  v  h  d  t  g  u  s  n  r  s  s  t  i  u  p  s  r
a  t  e  b  i  a  i  p  e  a  h  c  o  h  i  v  p  o  e  o
e  m  o  r  i  t  u  r  i  t  e  s  a  l  u  t  a  n  t  d
s  s  t  i  m  o  h  m  o  i  r  e  s  a  n  i  r  s  b  i
a  p  p  a  m  s  t  e  x  o  p  u  p  u  p  i  u  c  o  i
r  n  r  d  e  o  i  t  a  a  l  r  c  u  o  p  m  r  n  m
i  s  o  i  e  l  t  i  s  t  a  o  n  d  r  p  u  u  o  m
m  e  c  e  v  e  s  p  a  s  r  g  a  s  i  u  i  d  a  o
e  b  e  s  t  i  a  r  i  i  m  u  u  t  h  l  p  e  n  r
r  i  r  n  s  i  l  a  l  r  u  a  m  a  c  v  i  l  i  t
i  m  t  a  q  u  n  n  c  o  i  r  a  f  o  i  t  i  m  a
d  e  o  t  q  u  o  d  i  e  l  o  c  f  l  n  i  t  o  l
i  r  h  a  a  c  r  i  t  e  r  s  h  a  m  a  r  a  e  e
a  o  a  l  m  t  d  u  e  s  l  p  i  o  b  r  v  s  s
n  i  b  i  c  e  r  m  i  t  u  r  a  d  e  a  t  i  o  t
i  l  e  s  e  r  g  c  i  m  p  e  t  u  s  u  r  i  u  e
m  t  o  e  p  b  e  s  t  i  a  e  l  d  i  m  c  e  r  m
```

1. Colosseum	7. midday fighters	14. Bread and circuses!
2. Hail Caesar!	8. doll (*gen. pl.*)	15. attack (*noun*)
3. Those who are about to die greet you.	9. beast fighters	16. fiercely
4. games	10. Good heavens!	17. really
5. birthday	11. wild-beast hunt	18. Cheer up!
6. imperial seat of honor	12. sea fight	19. I am sure.
	13. wild animals	20. cruelty

CHAPTER 50 | NOTHING EVER HAPPENS

Activity 50a
Change each imperfect subjunctive to pluperfect and each pluperfect subjunctive to imperfect, keeping the same person, number, and voice:

1. inciperēs _____

2. admīrārentur (fem.) _____

3. incessissem _____

4. ostentus esset _____

5. māllēmus _____

6. laesae essēmus _____

7. sēnsisset _____

8. lāpsa essent _____

9. tergērēris (masc.) _____

10. repeterem _____

Activity 50b
Change each present subjunctive to perfect and each perfect subjunctive to present, keeping the same person, number, and voice:

1. mittās _____

2. cognōscātur (neut.) _____

3. subsequantur (fem.) _____

4. exsiluerit _____

5. velint _____

6. spectāverimus _____

7. habeātis _____

8. ierit _____

9. māluerim _____

10. tollāmus _____

Activity 50c
Fill in the blanks to match the English cues:

1. Cornēlia nōn intellegit cūr Eucleidēs verbum nūllum sibi _____. (says)

2. Cornēlia nōn intellegit cūr Eucleidēs verbum nūllum sibi _____. (said)

3. Cornēlia nōn intellēxit cūr Eucleidēs verbum nūllum sibi _____.
   (was saying)

(continued)

4. Cornēlia nōn intellēxit cūr Eucleidēs verbum nūllum sibi _____. (had said)

5. Cornēlia mīrābātur quid _____. (was happening)

6. Cornēlia mīrābātur quid _____. (had happened)

7. Cornēlia nōn rogat cūr pater sē Valeriō _____. (is promising)

8. Cornēlia nōn rogāvit cūr pater sē Valeriō _____. (had promised)

9. Cornēlia nōn rogāvit cūr pater sē Valeriō _____. (was promising)

10. Cornēlia nōn rogat cūr pater sē Valeriō _____. (promised)

Activity 50d
Fill in the blanks to match the English cues:

1. Tālis iuvenis est Valerius ut Cornēliō _____ fīliam eī dēspondēre. (it pleases)

2. Tālis iuvenis erat Valerius ut Cornēliō _____ (or _____) fīliam eī dēspondēre. (it pleased)

3. Pater tam gravī vultū loquitur ut Cornēlia _____ quid acciderit. (wonders)

4. Pater tam gravī vultū locūtus est ut Cornēlia _____ (or _____) quid accidisset. (wondered)

5. Cornēlia tam perturbāta erat ut vix loquī _____ (or _____). (was able)

6. Cornēlia adeō perturbāta est ut submissā vōce _____. (she replies)

7. Cornēlia adeō perturbāta erat ut submissā vōce _____ (or _____). (she replied)

8. Cornēlia tam laeta est ut vix loqui _____. (is able)

9. Cornēlia tam laeta erat ut vix loquī _____ (or _____). (was able)

10. Cornēlia tam laeta subitō facta est ut omnia Flāviae nārrāre _____ (or _____). (desired)

Activity 50e

Translate into English:

1. Veterēs Graecī ānulum in digitō sinistrae manūs quī minimō est proximus habuērunt.

_____

2. Rōmānī quoque ānulīs sīc plērumque ūsī sunt.

_____

3. Ōlim in Aegyptō medicī nervum tenuissimum ab eō digitō ad cor pergentem invēnērunt.

_____

_____

4. Nōn īnscītum igitur vīsum est ānulō in eō digitō ūtī, quī conexus esse cum corde vidēbātur.

_____

_____

plērumque, adv., *on many occasions, generally*

ūtor, ūtī, ūsus sum + abl., *to use/wear*

tenuis, -is, -e, *thin*

cor, cordis, n., *heart*

pergō, pergere, perrēxī, perrēctūrus, *to go on (to)*

īnscītus, -a, -um, *unreasonable*

conectō, conectere, conexuī, conexus, *to join, connect*

Activity 50f
Fill in the blanks. You may consult Latin and English dictionaries in doing this activity.

1. The Latin noun **coniūnx, coniugis,** m./f., means _____ or _____.
   It is a compound of the prefix **con-,** meaning _____, and the base **iug-** or
   iung-, meaning "yoke" or "to join by yoking," which is seen in the Latin words_____
   and _____. From the Latin word **coniūnx** is derived the English
   word *conjugal*, which means _____.

2. The English word *consort* is derived from the Latin prefix **con-,** meaning _____,
   and the Latin noun **sors, sortis,** f., meaning _____. The English word
   consort means _____or _____ , and is especially used of the
   spouse of a _____.

3. The Latin word **uxor, uxōris,** f., means _____. The English adjective
   uxorial means _____; the English adjective *uxorious* has a
   pejorative meaning: _____.

4. The English words *dower* and *dowry* are derived through Middle English and Old
   French from the Latin word _____. A dowry is _____
   _____.

5. The Latin noun **marītus, -ī,** m., means _____. From it is derived the English
   word *marital*, meaning _____. Also derived from **marītus** and its
   related Latin verb **marīto, -āre,** by way of Middle English and Old French is the
   English verb_____ and the English noun _____.

6. From the Latin noun **mātrimōnium, -ī,** n., meaning _____, is derived
   the English word _____. This word is applied to the state of being
   married and often refers to the _____aspects of marriage or the
   marriage rites.

7. The Latin verb **nūbō, nūbere, nūpsī, nūptūrus** means _____. From it
   are derived the English adjective *connubial*, meaning _____,
   and the English noun *nuptials*, meaning _____.
   The English adjective *nuptial* means _____.

8. From the Latin verb **spondeō, spondēre, spopondī, spōnsus,** meaning
   _____, is derived the English word *spouse*, meaning
   _____. Also derived from the Latin verb **spondeō** is the
   English verb *espouse*, meaning specifically _____ and more
   generally _____, as in the
   sentence, "He finally espoused the cause of justice."

9. Some English words having to do with marriage are derived from Old English and
   Anglo-Saxon rather than Latin. Thus, *betroth*, meaning _____
   or _____ is derived from the Old English word *treowth*, meaning
   _____. The English word *troth* is derived from this same Old English word and
   means _____. The Old English word
   wedd, meaning "a pledge," gave us the modern English verb _____ and the
   noun _____. This noun is used to refer to the legal rather than the
   religious aspect of marriage.

CHAPTER 51 | MARCUS COMES OF AGE

Activity 51a

Complete the indirect commands in the following sentences by supplying the correct form of the verb in parentheses. In each pair of sentences, the subordinate clause is first in primary and then in seconday sequence:

1. a. Cornēlius amīcōs clientēsque invītat ut domum suam crās _____. (venīre)

   b. Cornēlius amīcōs clientēsque invītāvit ut domum suam crās _____.(venīre)

2. a. Iānitor aliōs appropinquantēs rogat ut in domum _____. (prōcēdere)

   b. Iānitor aliōs appropinquantēs rogāvit ut in domum _____. (prōcēdere)

3. a. Iānitor aliīs domuī appropinquantibus praecipit ut in viā _____. (manēre)

   b. Iānitor aliīs domuī appropinquantibus praecipiēbat ut in viā _____(manēre)

4. a. Hī iānitōrem ōrant nē sē _____. (dīmittere)

   b. Hī iānitōrem ōrāvērunt nē sē _____. (dīmittere)

5. a. Iānitor eīs imperat ut statim _____. (discēdere)

   b. Iānitor eīs imperāvit ut statim _____. (discēdere)

6. a. Cornēlius omnēs domum intrantēs rogat ut in ātrium _____. (venīre)

   b. Cornēlius omnēs domum intrantēs rogāvit ut in ātrium _____. (venīre)

7. a. Cornēlius servō imperat ut togam pūram Marcō _____. (induere)

   b. Cornēlius servō imperāvit ut togam pūram Marcō _____. (induere)

8. a. Cornēlius eōs quī sē comitantur rogat ut extrā Tabulārium _____. (manēre)

   b. Cornēlius eōs quī sē comitābantur rogāvit ut extrā Tabulārium _____. (manēre)

9. a. Cornēlius multōs invītat ut apud sē hodiē _____. (cēnāre)

   b. Cornēlius multōs invītāvit ut apud sē hodiē _____. (cēnāre)

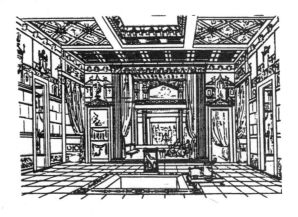

Activity 51b

Match each word at the left with a word at the right that is approximately the opposite in meaning. Give the meaning of each word.

1. lībertus (c) _____

2. benevolentia (d) _____

3. conticēscō (a) _____

4. imperō (f) _____

5. nōnnūllī (b) _____

6. praecipiō (e) _____

a. clāmō _____

b. complūrēs _____

c. servus _____

d. malevolentia _____

e. discō _____

f. pāreō _____

Activity 51c

Match each word at the left with a word at the right that is approximately the same in meaning. Give the meaning of each word.

1. sūmō (c) _____

2. ōrō (i) _____

3. imperō (d) _____

4. conticēscō (h) _____

5. amplector (a) _____

6. nōnnūllī (b) _____

7. praecipiō (g) _____

8. iānitor (f) _____

9. ergā (e) _____

a. complexū teneō _____

b. complūrēs _____

c. induō _____

d. iubeō _____

e. ad _____

f. custōs _____

g. doceō _____

h. taceō _____

i. obsecrō _____

CHAPTER 52

PAPIRIUS PRAETEXTATUS

Activity 52a

The following is the complete and unadapted story of Papirius Praetextatus as told by the Roman author Aulus Gellius. Write translations of each of the sections below. You may use the vocabulary at the end of *Pastimes and Ceremonies* in addition to the vocabulary and aids that are given with each Latin passage below. Write your translations on a separate sheet or sheets of paper.

1. Mōs anteā senātōribus Rōmae fuit in Cūriam cum praetextātīs fīliīs introīre. Tum, cum in senātū rēs maior quaepiam cōnsultāta eaque in diem posterum prōlāta est placuitque ut eam rem super quā tractāvissent nē quis ēnūntiāret priusquam dēcrēta esset, māter Papiriī puerī, quī cum parente suō in Cūriā fuerat, percontāta est fīlium quidnam in senātū patrēs ēgissent.

quispiam, quaepiam, quodpiam, *some, a certain*
cōnsultō, -āre, -āvī, -ātus, *to discuss* (with **cōnsultāta,** supply **est**)
super, prep. + abl., *about, concerning*
tractō, -āre, -āvī, -ātus, *to handle, deal with; to carry on a discussion*
priusquam, conj., *before*
dēcernō, dēcernere, dēcrēvī, dēcrētus, *to settle, decide*
percontor, -ārī, -ātus sum, *to question, ask*
quisnam, quaenam, quidnam, *who, what* (often introducing direct or indirect questions)

2. Puer respondit tacendum esse neque id dīcī licēre. Mulier fit audiendī cupidior; sēcrētum reī et silentium puerī animum eius ad inquīrendum ēverberat; quaerit igitur compressius violentiusque. Tum puer, mātre urgente, lepidī atque fēstīvī mendāciī cōnsilium capit.

tacendum esse, *that he must keep quiet*
audiendī, *of hearing*
cupidus, -a, -um + gen., *desirous (of)*
sēcrētum, -ī, n., *secret*
inquīrō, inquīrere, inquīsīvī, inquīsītus, *to inquire*
  ad inquīrendum, *for asking, to ask*
ēverberō, -āre, -āvī, -ātus, *to beat, stir up*
compressius, comparative of **compressē,** adv., *forcefully, urgently*
violentius, comparative of **violenter,** adv., *violently*
lepidus, -a, -um, *charming*
fēstīvus, -a, -um, *festive, witty*
mendācium, -ī, n., *falsehood*

3. Āctum in senātū dīxit utrum vidērētur ūtilius exque rē pūblicā esse ūnusne ut duās uxōrēs habēret an ut ūna apud duōs nūpta esset. Hoc illa ubi audīvit, animus compavēscit, domō trepidāns ēgreditur, ad cēterās mātrōnās perfert.

ūtilis, -is, -e, *useful*
ex, prep. + abl., here, *in accord with, in the interests of*
rēs pūblica, reī pūblicae, f., *the state, the public good*
-ne . . . an: these particles correlate the two parts of the double question; do not translate **-ne; an** = *or*
nūbō, nūbere, nūpsī, nūptūrus, *to marry*
compavēscō, compavēscere, *to become fearful*

4. Vēnit ad senātum postrīdiē mātrum familiās caterva. Lacrimantēs atque obsecrantēs ōrant ūna potius ut duōbus nūpta fieret quam ut ūnī duae. Senātōrēs, ingredientēs in Cūriam, quae illa mulierum intemperiēs et quid sibi postulātiō istaec vellet, mīrābantur.

māter familiās, mātris familiās, f., *mistress of a household, matron* (**familiās** is an old, archaic genitive singular of **familia**)

caterva, -ae, f., *flock, crowd*

intemperiēs, intemperiēī, f., *intemperate/outrageous behavior*

postulātiō, postulātiōnis, f., *demand, request*

istaec: an emphatic **ista**

volō, here, *to mean* (often used in this sense with **sibi,** *for itself,* which need not be translated). The direct objects of **vellet** are the interrogative pronouns **quae,** *what things,* and **quid,** *what.* The indirect questions depend on **mīrābantur,** *they were wondering. . . .*

5. Puer Papirius in medium Cūriae prōgressus, quid māter audīre īnstitisset, quid ipse mātrī dīxisset, rem, sīcut fuerat, dēnārrat. Senātus fidem atque ingenium puerī exōsculātur, cōnsultum facit utī posthāc puerī cum patribus in Cūriam nē introeant, praeter ille ūnus Papirius, atque puerō posteā cognōmentum honōris grātiā inditum "Praetextātus" ob tacendī loquendīque in aetāte praetextae prūdentiam.

īnstō, īnstāre, īnstitī, *to press urgently, be insistent*

sīcut, adv., *just as*

exōsculor, -ārī, -ātus sum, *to kiss; to express strong admiration for*

utī = ut. Note **utī . . . nē = nē,** *that . . . not*

posthāc, adv., *after this*

praeter: adverb, not a preposition, here

grātiā + preceding gen., *for the sake of*

indō, indere, indidī, inditus, *to give, bestow* (with **inditum** supply **est**)

ob, prep. + acc., *on account of, as a reward for*

tacendī loquendīque, *of keeping quiet and of speaking* (the genitives depend on **prūdentiam**)

aetās, aetātis, f., *age, time of life*

Activity 52b
Answer the following questions in English on a separate sheet or sheets of paper:

1. What words in the second passage above tell us the most about the character and personality of Papirius' mother? What kind of person is she?

2. Papirius tells his mother a blunt lie. How, in the second passage above, does the narrator try to put a good face on this action?

3. What words in the third and fourth passages above show the feelings and emotions of Papirius' mother and of the other women? What one word best characterizes the women's behavior? What sort of bias does the use of this word reveal in the men of the day or the narrator?

4. What one verb in the fifth passage above best characterizes the senators' feelings about Papirius?

5. What three qualities of character or personality do the senators admire in Papirius? Cite the three Latin nouns that express these qualities.

6. Was Papirius' mother wrong to insist so vehemently that her own son tell her the secret? Was Papirius right to tell his mother a lie?

7. How are the roles and character of the women in this story distinguished from those of the men?

8. The author of this story describes it as **iūcunda,** *entertaining.* Is there anything more to the story than mere entertainment? If so, what?

Activity 52c

Translate the following pairs of sentences:

1. **a.** Cornēliam urbis taedet. Ad vīllam rūsticam regredī vult.

   _____

   b. Flavia is tired of the country house and farm. She wants to go to Rome.

   _____

2. **a.** "Tē oportet tuam cistam parāre, sī Rōmam īre vīs," inquit Flāvius.

   _____

   b. Flavia and Vinia ought to go to Rome immediately, for Vinia will be the bride's attendant.

   _____

3. **a.** Cornēlius Cornēliam rogat: "Placetne tibi Valerium tē in mātrimōnium dūcere?"

   _____

   b. Vinia asks: "Does it please you to remain in Rome, Flavia?"

   _____

4. **a.** Spōnsum decet ānulum aureum tertiō digitō sinistrae manūs spōnsae aptāre.

   _____

   b. The groom should also give his bride a kiss.

   _____

5. **a.** Flāvia laetissima rogat: "Licetne mihi Rōmae manēre?"

   _____

   b. "You may if it pleases (you)," says her mother.

   _____

Activity 52d

The following Latin words are all connected with *augury*. Using a Latin dictionary, find definitions for the following:

1. dīvīnātiō, dīvīnātiōnis, f. _____

2. augur, auguris, m. _____

   _____

3. augurium, -ī, n.   a. _____

   b. _____

4. auspex, auspicis, m. _____

5. auspicium, -ī, n.   a. _____

   b. _____

6. haruspex, haruspicis, m. _____

7. haruspicium, -ī, n. _____

8. exta, -ōrum, n. pl. _____

9. extispex, extispicis, m. _____

_____

10. mōnstrum, -ī, n.   **a.** _____

_____

b. _____

11. prōdigium, -ī, n. _____

_____

12. ōmen, ōminis, n. _____

13. prōcūrātiō, prōcūrātiōnis, f. _____

_____

Activity 52e

The following English words are related to Latin words in Activity 52d above. Using an English dictionary as necessary, give definitions for the following:

1. divination: _____

2. divining rod: _____

_____

3. augury: _____

4. inaugurate: _____

5. to augur well: _____

6. auspices: _____

7. auspicious: _____

_____

8. monster: **a.** _____

b. _____

c. _____

9. prodigy: **a.** _____

b. _____

10. prodigious: _____

11. ill-omened: _____

12. ominous: _____

13. abominable: _____

CHAPTER 53

CORNELIA'S WEDDING

Activity 53a
Complete the purpose clauses in the following sentences by supplying the correct form of the verb that is given in its infinitive form in parentheses:

1. **a.** Ancillae hūc illūc concursant ut omnia _____. (parāre)

   b. Ancillae hūc illūc concursābant ut omnia _____. (parāre)

2. **a.** Auspex prōcēdit ut porcum _____. (sacrificāre)

   b. Auspex prōcessit ut porcum _____. (sacrificāre)

3. **a.** Nova nūpta super līmen tollitur nē _____. (lābī)

   b. Nova nūpta super līmen sublāta est nē _____. (lābī)

4. **a.** Multī amīcī conveniunt ut novae nūptae _____. (grātulārī)

   b. Multī amīcī convēnērunt ut novae nūptae _____. (grātulārī)

5. **a.** Iānitor baculum habet ut eōs quī neque amīcī neque propinquī sint _____.
   (repellere)

   b. Iānitor baculum habuit ut eōs quī neque amīcī neque propinquī essent_____.
   (repellere)

6. **a.** Marcus ante Larārium stat ut bullam Laribus _____. (cōnsecrāre)

   b. Marcus ante Larārium stābat ut bullam Laribus _____. (cōnsecrāre)

7. **a.** Amīcī cavēre dēbent nē _____. (cadere)

   b. Amīcī cavēre dēbēbant nē _____. (cadere)

8. **a.** Ancilla in cubiculum festīnat ut Cornēliae speculum _____. (dare)

   b. Ancilla in cubiculum festīnāvit ut Cornēliae speculum _____. (dare)

9. **a.** Servus vestīmenta custōdit nē quis ea _____. (surripere)

   b. Servus vestīmenta custōdīvit nē quis ea _____. (surripere)

10. **a.** Flāvia Rōmam venit ut Cornēliam _____. (adiuvāre)

    b. Flāvia Rōmam vēnit ut Cornēliam _____. (adiuvāre)

11. **a.** Eucleidēs per viās festīnat nē ā praedōnibus _____. (capī)

    b. Eucleidēs per viās festīnāvit nē ā praedōnibus _____. (capī)

12. **a.** Pater Sextī Rōmam redit ut filium sēcum domum _____. (dūcere)

    b. Pater Sextī Rōmam rediit ut filium sēcum domum _____. (dūcere)

13. **a.** Marcus ad Tabulārium dēdūcitur ut nōmen eius in tabulīs pūblicīs _____.
    (īnscrībī)

    b. Marcus ad Tabulārium dēductus est ut nōmen eius in tabulīs pūblicīs _____.
    (īnscrībī)

Activity 53b

The following is the story of Arria and her ill husband as told by Pliny (*Letters* III.16).
Write translations of both of the sections below. You may use the vocabulary at the
end of *Pastimes and Ceremonies* in addition to the vocabulary and aids that are given
with each Latin passage below. Write your translations on a separate sheet or sheets
of paper.

1. Aegrōtābat Caecina Paetus marītus Arriae, aegrōtābat et fīlius, uterque mortiferē, ut
vidēbātur. Fīlius dēcessit eximiā pulchritūdine parī verēcundiā, et parentibus nōn minus ob
alia cārus quam quod fīlius erat. Huic illa ita fūnus parāvit, ita dūxit exsequiās, ut ignōrāret
marītus; quīn immō quotiēns cubiculum eius intrāret, vīvere fīlium atque etiam
commodiōrem esse simulābat, ac persaepe interrogantī quid ageret puer, respondēbat,
"Bene quiēvit, libenter cibum sūmpsit."

pār, paris, *equal*

verēcundia, -ae, f., *modesty*

  eximiā pulchritūdine parī verēcundiā: two descriptive ablative phrases with the
    connective **et** omitted (asyndeton)

ob, prep. + acc., *on account of*

quīn immō, adv., *indeed*

quotiēns + subjn., *as often as, whenever*

commodus, -a, -um, *in good health*

persaepe, adv., *very often*

2. Deinde, cum diū cohibitae lacrimae vincerent prōrumperentque, ēgrediēbātur; tunc sē
dolōrī dabat; satiāta siccīs oculīs compositō vultū redībat, tamquam orbitātem forīs
relīquisset. Abdidit lacrimās, operuit luctum, āmissōque fīliō mātrem adhūc agēbat.

cohibeō, -ēre, -uī, -itus, *to hold back, restrain*

tunc, adv., *then*

satiō, -āre, -āvī, -ātus, *to satisfy, satiate*

orbitās, orbitātis, f., *loss (of a child)*

forīs, adv., *outside the door*

abdō, abdere, abdidī, abditus, *to put away, hide*

luctus, -ūs, m., *grief, mourning*

āmittō, āmittere, āmīsī, āmissus, *to lose*

Activity 53c

On a separate sheet of paper, write an essay in which you describe the character
of Arria as revealed in the passages in Activity 53b above, and contrast Arria's
character with that of the mother of Papirius and the other women in the passages
in Activity 52a.

CHAPTER 54 | A SAD OCCASION

Activity 54a

The following is a letter (V.16) written by Pliny to a friend concerning the recent death of the daughter of a mutual friend. Write translations of each of the sections below. You may use the vocabulary at the end of *Pastimes and Ceremonies* in addition to the vocabulary and aids that are given with each Latin passage. Write your translations on a separate sheet or sheets of paper.

C. PLINIUS AEFULANO MARCELLINO SUO S.

1. Trīstissimus haec tibi scrībō, Fundānī nostrī fīliā minōre dēfūnctā. Quā puellā nihil umquam fēstīvius amābilius, nec modo longiōre vītā sed prope immortālitāte dignius vīdī.

AEFULANO MARCELLINO: nothing is known about Aefulanus Marcellinus, the recipient of this letter.

G. Minicius Fundānus, -ī, m., *Gaius Minicius Fundanus* (a close friend of Pliny's and consul in A.D. 107)

fīlia: her name was Minicia Marcella.

minor, minor, minus, gen. **minōris,** *younger, smaller*

dēfungor, dēfungī, dēfūnctus sum, *to bring to an end; to die*

fēstīvus, -a, -um, *festal, congenial, happy*

amābilis, -is, -e, *lovable, delightful*

Note the lack of a connective (**et**) between the two adjectives (asyndeton).

nec modo . . . sed prope, *and not only . . . but almost . . .*

dignus, -a, -um + abl., *worthy of*

2. Nōndum annōs XIIII implēverat, et iam illī anīlis prūdentia, mātrōnālis gravitās erat et tamen suāvitās puellāris cum virginālī verēcundiā. Ut illa patris cervīcibus inhaerēbat! Ut nōs amīcōs paternōs et amanter et modestē complectēbātur! Ut nūtrīcēs, ut paedagōgōs, ut praeceptōrēs prō suō quemque officiō dīligēbat! Quam studiōsē, quam intelligenter lectitābat! Ut parcē custōdītēque lūdēbat!

Annōs XIIII: the girl's actual funerary urn and inscription were found outside Rome; the inscription gives her age as 12 (almost 13) years: **D(īs) M(ānibus) Miniciae Marcellae Fundānī f(īliae). V(īxit) a(nnōs) XII m(ēnsēs) XI d(iēs) VII.**

impleō, implēre, implēvī, implētus, *to fill* (used with **annōs** to express a person's age)

Illī: dative of possession (*there was for her = she had*)

anīlis, -is, -e, *belonging to/characteristic of an old woman* (**anus, -ūs,** f.)

verēcundia, -ae, f. *modesty*

Ut . . . ! *How . . . !*

cervīx, cervīcis, f., *neck* (plural for singular)

inhaereō, inhaerēre, inhaesī, inhaesūrus + dat., *to cling to*

modestē, adv., *modestly*

complector, complectī, complexus sum, *to embrace*

nūtrīx, nūtrīcis, f., *nurse* (of a child), *wet-nurse*

praeceptor, praeceptōris, m., *teacher, tutor* (here perhaps of private tutors, as Pliny remarks of a boy in another letter: **praeceptōrēs domī habuit,** III.3)

prō, prep. + abl., *according to*

quemque, *each*

studiōsē, adv., *eagerly*

intelligenter, adv., *intelligently*

lectitō, -āre, -āvī, -ātus, *to read frequently/repeatedly, to be in the habit of reading*

parcē, adv., *moderately, carefully*

lūdō, lūdere, lūsī, lūsūrus, *to play; to speak playfully, jest, joke*

3. Quā illa temperantiā, quā patientiā, quā etiam cōnstantiā novissimam valētūdinem tulit! Medicīs obsequēbātur, sorōrem patrem adhortābātur ipsamque sē dēstitūtam corporis vīribus vigōre animī sustinēbat. Dūrāvit hic illī usque ad extrēmum, nec aut spatiō valētūdinis aut metū mortis īnfrāctus est, quō plūrēs graviōrēsque nōbīs causās relinqueret et dēsīderiī et dolōris.

Quā . . . ! *(With) what . . . !*

temperantia, -ae, f., *self-control*

cōnstantia, -ae, f., *firmness, resolution*

obsequor, obsequī, obsecūtus sum + dat., *to follow* (a person's instructions)

dēstitūtus, -a, -um + abl., *deprived of*

sustineō, sustinēre, sustinuī, sustentus, *to support, sustain*

dūrō, -āre, -āvī, -ātus, *to last, remain*

hic: i.e., her **vigor animī**

usque ad + acc., *clear up to*

extrēmum, -ī, n., *end*

spatium, -ī, n., *length*

īnfringō, īnfringere, īnfrēgī, īnfrāctus, *to weaken, break, crush*

quō = ut, here introducing a result clause containing comparative adjectives

dēsiderium, -ī, n., *longing, desire* (as for a dead person)

4. Ō trīste plānē acerbumque fūnus! Ō morte ipsā mortis tempus indignius! Iam dēstināta erat ēgregiō iuvenī, iam ēlēctus nūptiārum diēs, iam nōs vocātī. Quod gaudium quō maerōre mūtātum est! Nōn possum exprimere verbīs quantum animō vulnus accēperim, cum audīvī Fundānum ipsum, ut multa lūctuōsa dolor invēnit, praecipientem, quod in vestēs margarīta gemmās fuerat ērogātūrus, hoc in tūs et unguenta et odōrēs impenderētur.

plānē, adv., *plainly, utterly, absolutely*

acerbus, -a, -um, *bitter, distressing, untimely, premature* (of death)

indignus, -a, -um, *unworthy, cruel, shocking*

dēstinō, -āre, -āvī, -ātus, *to destine, engage* (by formal arrangement). Girls could be promised and given in marriage as young as 12 years of age.

ēgregius, -a, -um, *outstanding, excellent*

ēligō, ēligere, ēlēgī, ēlēctus, *to select, choose*

gaudium, -ī, n., *joy*

maeror, maerōris, m., *grief, sorrow, mourning*

mūtō, -āre, -āvī, -ātus + acc. and abl., *to exchange* (one thing, acc.) *for* (another, abl.)

ut multa . . . dolor invēnit! *as (his) grief found many . . . !*

lūctuōsus, -a, -um, *sorrowful, mournful*

praecipientem, *instructing, ordering* (introducing an indirect command with its verb, **impenderētur,** in the subjunctive but with the usual **ut** omitted)

quod, *that (money) which*

margarītum, -ī, n., *pearl*

gemma, -ae, f., *gem*

ērogō, -āre, -āvī, -ātus, *to pay*

tūs, tūris, n., *frankincense* (used in funeral ceremonies)

odor, odōris, m., *perfume* (used in funeral ceremonies)

impendō, impendere, impendī, impēnsus, *to spend*

(continued)

5. Est quidem ille ērudītus et sapiēns, ut quī sē ab ineunte aetāte altiōribus studiīs
   artibusque dēdiderit; sed nunc omnia, quae audiit saepe quae dīxit, aspernātur
   expulsīsque virtūtibus aliīs pietātis est tōtus. Ignōscēs, laudābis etiam, si cōgitāveris
   quid āmīserit.

sapiēns, sapientis, *wise, philosophical.* This was the term for a Stoic philosopher, "sage,"
   or "wise man." The Stoic school of philosophy taught that the "wise man" would
   always be in full control of his emotions. Minicius may have attended the philosophical
   school of the famous Stoic philosopher Musonius Rufus.

ut quī + subjn.; a relative clause with the subjunctive is used to describe a characteristic
   of the antecedent: *he is . . . wise,* (someone) *who (characteristically) devotes himself to. . . .*
   The addition of **ut** emphasizes cause: *since (he is the sort of person) who devotes himself
   to. . . .* **Ut quī** may thus be translated simply *since he. . . .*

aetās, aetātis, f., *age*

   ab ineunte aetāte, *from earliest youth*

ars, artis, gen. pl., **artium,** f., *skill, art;* pl., *liberal arts*

dēdō, dēdere, dēdidī, dēditus + dat., *to devote* (oneself) *to.* What tense of the
   subjunctive is **dēderit** and why?

audiit = audīvit

saepe: understand with both **audiit** and **dīxit.** Note the lack of connective (asyndeton)
   between the two relative clauses.

aspernor, -ārī, -ātus sum, *to reject*

virtūs, virtūtis, f., *virtue, moral excellence.* Here the word may refer to the qualities of
   moral character such as resolution and control over emotions that were taught by the
   Stoic philosophers.

pietās, pietātis, f.: this word and the concept it embodies defy simple translation into
   English. **Pietās** was an attitude of respect toward others; here it is used of the respect,
   love, and compassion felt by the father for his daughter.

tōtus, -a, -um + gen., *totally given over to*

ignōscō, ignōscere, ignōvī, ignōtus + dat., *to pardon* (supply **eī,** *him,* as object)

cōgitāveris: what tense of the indicative is this, and why is this tense used here?

āmittō, āmittere, āmīsī, āmissus, *to lose.* What tense of the subjunctive is **āmīserit,** and
   in what kind of a clause is the subjunctive used here?

6. Āmīsit enim filiam, quae nōn minus mōrēs eius quam ōs vultumque referēbat, tōtumque
   patrem mīrā similitūdine excrīpserat. Proinde sī quās ad eum dē dolōre tam iūstō litterās
   mittēs, mementō adhibēre sōlācium nōn quasi castīgātōrium et nimis forte, sed molle et
   hūmānum.

exscrībō, exscrībere, exscrīpsī, exscrīptus, *to copy, resemble*

proinde (pronounce as two syllables), adv., *accordingly*

quās, *any*

iūstus, -a, -um, *lawful, legitimate, appropriate*

mementō (imperative), *remember*

adhibeō, adhibēre, adhibuī, adhibitus, *to provide, offer*

sōlācium, -ī, n., *consolation*

castīgātōrius, -a, -um, *containing criticism/reproof*

nimis forte, *too strong/severe*

mollis, -is, -e, *soft, gentle*

7. Quod ut facilius admittat, multum faciet mediī temporis spatium. Ut enim crūdum adhūc vulnus medentium manūs reformidat, deinde patitur atque ultrō requīrit, sīc recēns animī dolor cōnsōlātiōnēs rēicit ac refugit, mox dēsīderat et clēmenter admōtīs adquiēscit. Valē.

quod: i.e, the **sōlācium** contained in the letter that Aefulanus may send to Minicius

ut . . . admittat: this clause, expressing result, functions as the object of the verb **faciet** in the main clause: *will bring it about that. . . .*

admittō, admittere, admīsī, admissus, *to receive, accept*

spatium, -ī, n., *space, length*

ut . . . reformidat . . . patitur . . . requīrit: how is **ut** translated with the indicative?

crūdus, -a, -um, *raw*

medēns, medentis, gen. pl., **medentium,** m., *doctor*

reformidō, -āre, -āvī, -ātus, *to shrink back/recoil in fear from something*

ultrō, adv., *voluntarily*

requīrō, requīrere, requīsīvī, requīsītus, *to seek*

recēns, recentis, *recent, fresh*

rēiciō, rēicere, rēiēcī, rēiectus, *to refuse to accept; to reject*

refugiō, refugere, refūgī, *to shrink away from, shun, avoid*

admoveō, admovēre, admōvī, admōtus, *to bring, offer.* With **admōtīs** supply the noun **cōnsōlātiōnibus.** The participle **admōtīs** has a conditional force: *if offered. . . .*

adquiēscō, adquiēscere, adquiēvī + dat., *to find rest/relief in something*

Activity 54b

Referring to Activity 54a above, answer the following questions in English on a separate sheet or sheets of paper:

1. In passage no. 1, locate an example of hyperbole (exaggeration for rhetorical effect). How is the hyperbole here appropriate to the tone and purpose of this letter?

2. What characteristics of Minicia does Pliny find most remarkable in passage no. 2?

3. What is the rhetorical effect of the exclamations in passage no. 2?

4. Locate an example of asyndeton in passage no. 3.

5. Why has Minicia left "more and deeper causes of longing and grief" (passage no. 3)? What was it about her behavior that caused even greater longing and grief?

6. What further reason for sorrow is referred to in passage no. 4?

7. How does the metaphorical use of the word **vulnus** in passage no. 4 help Pliny express what he claims "not to be able to express in words"?

8. In passage no. 4 the phrase **in vestēs margarīta gemmās** is balanced by the phrase **in tūs et unguenta et odōrēs.** Can you think of any explanation of why Pliny uses asyndeton in the former list and not in the latter?

(continued)

9. What hints about the advanced education of Minicius are we given in passage no. 5? How does the education he has received differ from that received by his daughter (passage no. 2)?

10. What might be regarded as blameworthy in Minicius' behavior (passage no. 5)? How does Pliny defend him?

11. In passage no. 6 Pliny remarks on the similarity in character of daughter and father. What earlier indications are there in the letter that their characters were similar?

12. What will be necessary before Minicius will be able to accept even consolation that is gentle and humane (passage no. 7)?

13. Explain as fully as possible the comparison Pliny draws between a wound and grief (passage no. 7).

Activity 54c
Fill in the blanks. You may consult Latin and English dictionaries in doing this activity.

1. From the Latin noun **fūnus, fūneris,** n., are derived the English words *funeral* and *funereal.* The word *funeral* may be either a noun or an _____. The word *funereal* means either _____or, more generally, _____.

2. The Latin word **exsequiae, -ārum,** f. pl., gives the English word _____ , which means _____.

3. The English word *obsequies* also means _____and is derived from the Latin word **obsequia,** n. pl., which has a similar meaning.

4. The English words *lamentation* and *(to) lament* are derived from the Latin noun _____and the Latin verb _____, respectively.

5. The Latin noun **sepulcrum, -ī,** n., gives the English noun _____and the English adjective _____.

NOUNS

1st Declension

āra, -ae, f., *altar*
benevolentia, -ae, f., *kindness*
bulla, -ae, f., *luck-charm, locket*
candēla, -ae, f., *candle*
caterva, -ae, f., *crowd*
coxa, -ae, f., *hipbone*
dextra, -ae, f., *right hand*
epulae, -ārum, f. pl., *banquet, feast*
exsequiae, -ārum, f. pl., *funeral rites*
  exsequiās dūcere, *to carry out funeral rites*
familia, -ae, f., *family, household*
fortūna, -ae, f., *fortune (good or bad)*
harēna, -ae, f., *sand*
īnferiae, -ārum, f. pl., *offerings and rites in honor of the dead at the tomb*
līberta, -ae, f., *freedwoman*
lucerna, -ae, f., *lamp*
mātrōna, -ae, f., *married woman*
nātūra, -ae, f., *nature*
nēnia, -ae, f., *lament, dirge*
nova nūpta, -ae, f., *bride*
pompa, -ae, f., *procession*
prōnuba, -ae, f., *bride's attendant*
prūdentia, -ae, f., *good sense, discretion, skill*
serva, -ae, f., *slave-woman, slave-girl*
spōnsa, -ae, f., *betrothed woman, bride*
toga pūra, -ae, f., *plain white toga*
tabulae, -ārum, f. pl., *tablets, records*
taeda, -ae, f., *torch*
tunica alba, -ae, f., *white tunic (worn by brides)*
Via Flāminia, -ae, f., *the Via Flaminia (a road from Rome leading through the Campus Martius and north to Ariminum on the Adriatic Sea)*
vīta, -ae, f., *life*
  ē vītā excēdere, *to die*
vitta, -ae, f., *ribbon*

2nd Declension

ānulus, -ī, m., *ring*
capillī, -ōrum, m. pl., *hair*
  capillīs solūtīs, *with dishevelled hair*
concubīnus, -ī, m., *bridegroom*
cōnsultum, -ī, n., *decree*
exta, -ōrum, n. pl., *the inner organs of sacrifical animals (heart, lungs, liver)*
flammeum, -ī, n., *orange (bridal) veil*
hortulus, -ī, m., *small garden*
ingenium, -ī, n., *intelligence, ingenuity*
larārium, -ī, n., *shrine of the household gods*
laurus, -ī, f., *bay (tree), laurel*
marītus, -ī, m., *husband*
mātrimōnium, -ī, n., *marriage*
  in mātrimōnium dūcere, *to marry*
meritum, -ī, n., *good deed;* pl., *services*
  merita cōnferre, *to render services (to)*
mīmus, -ī, m., *actor of mime, buffoon*
modus, -ī, m., *way, method; rhythmic/harmonious manner*
monumentum, -ī, n., *monument, tomb*
morbus, -ī, m., *illness*
myrtus, -ī, f., *myrtle*
nātus, -ī, m., *son*
Ōceanus, -ī, m., *Ocean*
officium, -ī, n., *official ceremony, duty*
propinquus, -ī, m., *relative*
rogus, -ī, m., *funeral pyre*
sacra, -ōrum, n. pl., *religious rites, sacrifice*
spōnsus, -ī, m., *betrothed man, bridegroom*
Tabulārium, -ī, n., *Public Records Office*
Talassius, -ī, m., *Talassius (god of marriage)*

3rd Declension

āctor, āctōris, m., *actor*
aequor, aequoris, n., *sea*
appāritor, appāritōris, m., *gate-keeper, public servant*
aquilō, aquilōnis, m., *north wind*
auspex, auspicis, m., *augur, officiating priest*
avis, avis, gen. pl., **avium**, m./f., *bird*
cinis, cineris, m., *ashes, dust (of the cremated body)*
cognōmen, cognōminis, n., *surname (third or fourth name of a Roman)*
cor, cordis, n., *heart*
familiārēs, familiārium, m. pl., *members of the household*
fascēs, fascium, m. pl., *rods (symbols of office)*
fax, facis, f., *wedding-torch*
febris, febris, gen. pl., **febrium**, f., *fever*
fūnus, fūneris, n., *funeral*
gēns, gentis, gen. pl., **gentium**, f., *family, clan;* pl., *peoples*
hilaritās, hilaritātis, f., *good humor, merriment*
imāgō, imāginis, f., *likeness, mask*
iuvenis, iuvenis, m., *young man*
Larēs, Larum, m. pl., *household gods*
Līberālia, Līberālium, n. pl., *the Liberalia (Festival of Liber)*
līctor, līctōris, m., *lictor, officer*
līmen, līminis, n., *threshold, doorway*
  super līmen tollere, *to carry over the threshold*
maiōrēs, maiōrum, m. pl., *ancestors*
mānēs, mānium, m. pl., *spirits of the dead*
  dīs mānibus, *to the spirits of the dead*
morbus, -ī, m., *illness*
mōs, mōris, m., *custom;* pl., *character*
mūnus, mūneris, n., *gift, service, gladiatorial show;* pl., *games*
nux, nucis, f., *nut*
ōmen, ōminis, n., *omen*
os, ossis, n., *bone*
patrēs, patrum, m. pl., *senators*
pectus, pectoris, n., *chest, breast*
  pectus plangere, *to beat the breast*
pīstor, pīstōris, m., *baker*
pulchritūdō, pulchritūdinis, f., *beauty*
redēmptor, redēmptōris, m., *contractor*
sermō, sermōnis, m., *conversation, talk*
sōl, sōlis, m., *sun*

spōnsālia, spōnsālium, n. pl.,
    betrothal ceremony
    ad spōnsālia, *for the betrothal*
tībīcen, tībīcinis, m., *piper*
viscera, viscerum, n. pl., *vital organs*
vispillō, vispillōnis, m., *undertaker*

4th Declension
flētus, -ūs, m., *weeping, tears*
incessus, -ūs, m., *bearing, walk(ing)*

5th Declension
fidēs, fideī, f., *good faith, reliability,
    trust*

ADJECTIVES

1st and 2nd Declension
albus, -a, -um, *white*
cārus, -a, -um, *dear, beloved*
castus, -a, -um, *virtuous, chaste*
clārus, -a, -um, *bright*
comitātus, -a, -um, *accompanied*
commodus, -a, -um, *pleasant*
conversus, -a, -um, *having turned,
    turning*
dēditus, -a, -um, *devoted, dedicated*
eximius, -a, -um, *outstanding*
frāternus, -a, -um, *brotherly*
gelātus, -a, -um, *chilled*
grātus, -a, -um + dat., *loved (by),
    pleasing (to), dear (to)*
hyacinthinus, -a, -um, *of hyacinth*
iūcundus, -a, -um, *pleasant,
    delightful*
lepidus, -a, -um, *charming*
lūbricus, -a, -um, *slippery*
mūtus, -a, -um, *silent*
nōnnūllī, -ae, -a, *some*
officiōsus, -a, -um + dat., *ready to
    serve, obliging*
paulus, -a, -um, *little, small*
perpetuus, -a, -um, *lasting,
    permanent*
    in perpetuum, *forever*
perturbātus, -a, -um, *confused*
posterus, -a, -um, *next, following*
praetextātus, -a, -um, *wearing the
    toga praetexta*
prīscus, -a, -um, *of olden times,
    ancient*
pūblicus, -a, -um, *public*
pūrus, -a, -um, *spotless, clean,
    plain white*

serēnus, -a, -um, *clear, bright*
siccus, -a, -um, *dry*
sinister, sinistra, sinistrum, *left*
situs, -a, -um, *located, situated, buried*
subitus, -a, -um, *sudden*
submissus, -a, -um, *quiet, subdued,
    soft*
tantus, -a, -um, *so great*
varius, -a, -um, *different, varied,
    many-hued*
vectus, -a, -um, *having been carried,
    having traveled*

3rd Declension
familiāris, -is, -e, *belonging to the
    family/household*
fūnebris, -is, -e, *funeral*
hilaris, -is, -e, *cheerful*
iners, inertis, *lazy*
levis, -is, -e, *light*
lēvis, -is, -e, *smooth*
mollis, -is, -e, *soft*
nōbilis, -is, -e, *noble*
nūptiālis, -is, -e, *of/for a wedding*
puerīlis, -is, -e, *childish, of childhood*
similis, -is, -e + dat., *similar (to), like*
tālis, -is, -e, *such*
trepidāns, trepidantis, *in a panic*

Indeclinable
tot, *so many*

VERBS

1st Conjugation
adstō, adstāre, adstitī, *to stand near,
    stand by*
aptō, -āre, -āvī, -ātus, *to place, fit*
commemorō, -āre, -āvī, -ātus, *to
    mention, comment on, recount*
cōnsecrō, -āre, -āvī, -ātus, *to
    dedicate*
creō, -āre, -āvī, -ātus, *to appoint,
    create*
dōnō, -āre, -āvī, -ātus, *to give; to
    present somebody (acc.) with
    something (abl.)*
ēnūntiō, -āre, -āvī, -ātus, *to reveal,
    divulge*
imperō, -āre, -āvī, -ātus + dat., *to
    order*
interrogō, -āre, -āvī, -ātus, *to ask*
invītō, -āre, -āvī, -ātus, *to invite*
locō, -āre, -āvī, -ātus, *to place*
mānō, -āre, -āvī, *to flow*

nōminō, -āre, -āvī, -ātus, *to name,
    call by name*
obsecrō, -āre, -āvī, -ātus, *to beseech,
    beg*
observō, -āre, -āvī, -ātus, *to watch,
    pay attention to*
obsignō, -āre, -āvī, -ātus, *to sign*
optō, -āre, -āvī, -ātus, *to wish*
ornō, -āre, -āvī, -ātus, *to decorate,
    equip*
ōrō, -āre, -āvī, -ātus, *to beg*
plōrō, -āre, -āvī, -ātus, *to lament,
    mourn*
rogō, -āre, -āvī, -ātus, *to ask*
sacrificō, -āre, -āvī, -ātus, *to sacrifice*
violō, -āre, -āvī, -ātus, *to do harm*

2nd Conjugation
ārdeō, ārdēre, ārsī, ārsūrus, *to burn,
    blaze*
decet, decēre, decuit, *it is becoming,
    fitting; should*
    **Nōn decet patrem dēspondēre
    filiam**, *That a father should
    betroth his daughter is not fitting,
    A father should not betroth his
    daughter.*
**dēspondeō, dēspondēre, dēspondī,
    dēspōnsus**, *to betroth, promise in
    marriage*
fleō, flēre, flēvī, flētus, *to weep, cry*
langueō, -ēre, *to be ill in bed*
libet, libēre, libuit or **libitum est**, *it
    is pleasing to someone (dat.) to do
    something (infin.)*
licet, licēre, licuit + dat., *it is allowed*
lūcet, lūcēre, lūxit, *it is light, it is
    day; (it) shines*
moneō, -ēre, -uī, -itus, *to advise,
    warn*
oportet, oportēre, oportuit, *it is
    fitting; ought*
    Festīnāre tē oportet, *That you
    hurry is fitting, You ought to hurry.*
**persuādeō, persuādēre, persuāsī,
    persuāsus**, *to make something
    (acc.) agreeable to someone (dat.), to
    persuade someone of something; to
    persuade someone (dat.)*
placeō, -ēre, -uzī + dat., *to please*
    placuit, *it was decided*
praebeō, -ēre, -uī, -itus, *to display,
    show, provide*

spondeō, spondēre, spopondī, spōnsus, *to promise solemnly, pledge*

taedet, taedēre, taesum est, *it bores, makes one* (acc.) *tired of something* (gen.)
   mē taedet + gen., *it tires me of . . . , I tired (of), bored (with)*

urgeō, urgēre, ursī, *to press, insist*

3rd Conjugation

accendō, accendere, accendī, accēnsus, *to set on fire*

agō, agere, ēgī, āctus, *to do, drive; to discuss, debate*

āvertō, āvertere, āvertī, āversus, *to turn away, divert*

compōnō, compōnere, composuī, compositus, *to compose*

concinō, concinere, concinuī, *to sing together*

dēcēdō, dēcēdere, dēcessī, dēcessūrus, *to die*

dēdūcō, dēdūcere, dēdūxī, dēductus, *to show into, bring, escort*

dēmittō, dēmittere, dēmīsī, dēmissus, *to let down, lower*

dēsinō, dēsinere, dēsiī, dēsitus, *to stop*

dīligō, dīligere, dīlēxī, dīlēctus, *to love, have special regard for*

dīmittō, dīmittere, dīmīsī, dīmissus, *to send away*

ēruō, ēruere, ēruī, ērutus, *to dig up*

excēdō, excēdere, excessī, excessūrus, *to go out, leave*

eximō, eximere, exēmī, exēmptus, *to remove*

exstruō, exstruere, extrūxī, exstrūctus, *to build*

frangō, frangere, frēgī, frāctus, *to break*

impōnō, impōnere, imposuī, impositus, *to place on, put*

incidō, incidere, incidī, incāsūrus, *to fall into, fall onto*

ingravēscō, ingravēscere, *to grow worse*

īnscrībō, īnscrībere, īnscrīpsī, īnscrīptus, *to write in, register*

iungō, iungere, iūnxī, iūnctus, *to join*

linquō, linquere, līquī, *to leave*

neglegō, neglegere, neglēxī, neglēctus, *to neglect, ignore*

nūbō, nūbere, nūpsī, nūptūrus + dat., *to marry*

perlegō, perlegere, perlēgī, perlēctus, *to read through*

plangō, plangere, plānxī, plānctus, *to beat*

praecēdō, praecēdere, praecessī, praecessūrus, *to go in front*

prōrumpō, prōrumpere, prōrūpī, prōruptus, *to burst forth, burst out*

requīrō, requīrere, requīsīvī, requīsītus, *to ask, inquire*

rescrībō, rescrībere, rescrīpsī, rescrīptus, *to write back, reply*

scindō, scindere, scidī, scissus, *to cut, split, carve, tear*

solvō, solvere, solvī, solūtus, *to loosen, untie, dishevel*

sūmō, sūmere, sūmpsī, sūmptus, *to take, take up, pick out, assume (i.e., put on for the first time)*

tangō, tangere, tetigī, tāctus, *to touch*

tegō, tegere, tēxī, tēctus, *to cover*

vehō, vehere, vexī, vectus, *to carry;* pass., *to be carried, travel*

3rd Conjugation -iō

afficiō, afficere, affēcī, affectus, *to affect*

iniciō, inicere, iniēcī, iniectus, *to throw into, thrust*

praecipiō, praecipere, praecēpī, praeceptus + dat., *to instruct, order*

4th Conjugation

operiō, operīre, operuī, opertus, *to hide, cover*

serviō, -īre, -īvī, -ītūrus + dat., *to serve*

Irregular

cōnferō, cōnferre, contulī, collātus, *to confer, bestow*

introeō, introīre, introiī or introīvī, introitūrus, *to enter*

perferō, perferre, pertulī, perlātus, *to report*

prōdeō, prōdīre, prōdiī, prōditūrus, *to come forth*

prōferō, prōferre, prōtulī, prōlātus, *to carry forward, continue*

DEPONENT VERBS

1st Conjugation

comitor, -ārī, -ātus sum, *to accompany*

grātulor, -ārī, -ātus sum + dat., *to congratulate*

hortor, -ārī, -ātus sum, *to encourage, urge*

3rd Conjugation

alloquor, alloquī, allocūtus sum, *to speak to, address*

amplector, amplectī, amplexus sum, *to embrace*

PRONOUNS

aliquis, aliquid, *someone, something*
   nē quis (quis = aliquis), *that no one*
   sī quis (quis = aliquis), *if anyone*

tētē, emphatic tē

PREPOSITIONS

dē + abl., *down from, from, concerning, about*

ergā + acc., *toward*

super + acc., *over, above*

ADVERBS

adeō, *so much, to such an extent*

Fēlīciter! *Good luck!*

indignē, *undeservedly*

ita, *thus, in such a way*

mortiferē, *mortally, critically*

nēquīquam, *in vain*

nūper, *recently*

prōtinus, *immediately*

quandōquidem, *since*

rīte, *properly*

sīc, *thus, in this way*

tam, *so*

tantum, *so much*

CONJUNCTIONS

nē + subjunctive, *not to, so that . . .*
not, to prevent, to avoid
ut + subjunctive, *so that, that, to*
utrum . . . an . . ., *whether . . . or*

MISCELLANEOUS

ait, *(he/she) says, said*
causā, with genitive case preceding,
by way of, as
    honōris causā, *for the sake of an
honor, as an honor*
cūrae esse, *to be a cause of anxiety (to)*
eō magis, *all the more*
erat īnscrībendum, *had to be
registered*
est arcessendus, *must be sent for*
grātiās agere + dat., *to thank*

Heus! *Hey there!*
Hymēn! (an exclamation chanted at
weddings; later thought of as the
god of weddings)
Hymenaee! = Hymēn!
id quod, *that/a thing which*
in Forum dēdūcere, *to escort to the
Forum*
Iō! (a ritual exclamation)
potius quam, *rather than*

Activity XIIa

Translate into Latin, using the story in Exercise XIIg in *Pastimes and Ceremonies* as a guide:

1. It was decided to divide the supreme power among four commanders. (Use infinitive.)

2. It was decided that the supreme power be divided among four commanders. (Use an **ut** clause.)

3. The supreme power was divided so that the commanders might rule so many provinces more easily. (Use a purpose clause.)

4. Constantine escaped from his guards to go to his father (who was) affected with illness in Britain. (Use a purpose clause and a perfect passive participle.)

5. After his father has died, Constantine goes to Italy to make his power secure with arms. (Use an ablative absolute and a purpose clause.)

6. Constantine orders his soldiers to put the sign of the cross on their shields and helmets. (Use an indirect command.)

7. On account of his victory Constantine is so grateful that he keeps the cross as his sign. (Use a result clause.)

8. He proclaims the edict of Milan so that Christians may no longer be harassed/annoyed. (Use a negative purpose clause.)

9. Constantine thought that the empire ought to be ruled by one emperor. (Use **oportēre**.)

10. After Licinius had been defeated, Constantine moved the seat of empire from Rome to Byzantium and built a new city that he called Constantinople. (Use an ablative absolute.)

Activity XIIb

Fill in the spaces at the right with translations of the English at the left. When you are finished, copy the circled letters in order and you will discover a Latin *sententia*. Write its meaning in the space provided.

1. in a subdued voice   __ __ __ ◯ __ __ __ __   __ ◯ __ __

2. relatives (nom. pl.)   __ ◯ __ __ ◯ __ __ __ __

3. they were admiring   __ __ __ __ ◯ __ __ __ ◯ __

4. to thank   __ __ __ __ __ __ ◯ ◯ __ __ __ __

5. funeral (nom. sing.)   __ __ ◯ __ __

6. to encourage, urge   __ __ __ ◯ __ __ ◯

7. I grew quiet   ◯ ◯ __ __ __ ◯

8. fever   __ __ __ __ __ ◯

9. parents (acc. pl.)   __ __ ◯ __ __ __ ◯ ◯

10. standing near (nom. pl.)   __ __ ◯ ◯ ◯ __ __ __ __

11. on the next day   __ __ __ ◯ __ ◯ ◯ __ __ __

12. masks of ancestors   __ ◯ ◯ __ ◯ __ __ __ ◯ __ __ __ __

13. toga of manhood   __ __ __ __ ◯ ◯ ◯ ◯ __ __ ◯

14. they were talking together   __ __ __ __ __ ◯ ◯ __ __ __ __ __ __ __

15. funeral (adj.)   __ __ __ ◯ __ __ __ __

Copy circled letters here: __ __ __ __ __ __ __   __ __ __ __ __ __ __

__ __ __ __ __ __ __ __   __ __ __ __ __ __ __

Meaning of **sententia** _____

_____

SELECTIVE REVIEW

Passage 1

Trīstissimus haec tibi scrībō, Fundānī nostrī fīliā minōre dēfūnctā. Quā puellā nihil umquam fēstīvius amābilius, nec modo longiōre vītā sed prope immortālitāte dignius vīdī.

1. **Positive, Comparative, and Superlative of Adjectives.** Locate five comparative or superlative adjectives in the passage above, enter them in the appropriate columns, and fill in the other forms in the same gender, case, and number.

   Positive   *Comparative*   *Superlative*

   _____   _____   _____

   _____   _____   _____

   _____   _____   _____

   _____   _____   _____

   _____   _____   _____

   _____   _____   _____

   Locate one phrase that is in the ablative to express comparison: _____

2. **Genitive of Possession.** Copy here a phrase in the genitive expressing possession:

   _____

3. **Dative of Indirect Object.** Locate one dative indirect object: _____

4. **Ablative Absolute.** Copy one ablative absolute here: _____

   _____

   Translate the entire sentence in which it occurs:

   _____

   What tense is the participle in the ablative absolute? _____

5. **Ablative with Adjective.** Copy here the words in the ablative that go with the

   adjective *dignius, more worthy of:* _____ _____

Passage 2

Nōndum annōs XIIII implēverat, et iam illī anīlis prūdentia, mātrōnālis gravitās erat et tamen suāvitās puellāris cum virginālī verēcundiā. Ut illa patris cervīcibus inhaerēbat! Ut nōs amīcōs paternōs et amanter et modestē complectēbātur! Ut nūtrīcēs, ut paedagōgōs, ut praeceptōrēs prō suō quemque officiō dīligēbat! Quam studiōsē, quam intellegenter lectitābat! Ut parcē custōdītēque lūdēbat!

1. **Verbs.** Fill in the following chart with the forms of the following verbs in the 3rd person singular:

	impleō, implēre, implēvī, implētus		complector, complectī, complexus sum
		Indicative	
	Active	*Passive*	
Present	_____	_____	_____
Imperfect	_____	_____	_____

(continued)

	Active	Indicative Passive	
Future	_____	_____	_____
Perfect	_____	_____	_____
Pluperfect	_____	_____	_____
Future Perfect	_____	_____	_____
		Subjunctive	
Present	_____	_____	_____
Imperfect	_____	_____	_____
Perfect	_____	_____	_____
Pluperfect	_____	_____	_____

2. **Frequentative Verb.** Locate one frequentative verb in passage 2:

_____

3. **Nouns and Adjectives: Agreement.** Locate five phrases consisting of a noun and an adjective. Write them at the left and then identify their gender, number, and case:

	Gender	*Number*	*Case*
_____	_____	_____	_____
_____	_____	_____	_____
_____	_____	_____	_____
_____	_____	_____	_____
_____	_____	_____	_____

4. **The Demonstrative** *ille*. Locate two examples of this word in passage 2:

_____ _____

Is the word being used here as an adjective or a pronoun? (Circle *adjective* or *pronoun*.) Write the forms of this demonstrative adjective/pronoun in the singular:

	Masculine	*Feminine*	*Neuter*
Nom.	_____	_____	_____
Gen.	_____	_____	_____
Dat.	_____	_____	_____
Acc.	_____	_____	_____
Abl.	_____	_____	_____

5. **Dative Case with Compound Verb.** Locate one example of a noun in the dative case used with a compound verb; write the noun and verb here:

_____

6. **Adverbs.** Locate five adverbs that have positive, comparative, and superlative degrees; enter them in the appropriate columns, and fill in the other forms:

Positive   *Comparative*   *Superlative*

_____   _____   _____

_____   _____   _____

_____   _____   _____

_____   _____   _____

_____   _____   _____

_____   _____   _____

Passage 3

Quā illa temperantiā, quā patientiā, quā etiam cōnstantiā novissimam valētūdinem tulit! Medicīs obsequēbātur, sorōrem patrem adhortābātur ipsamque sē dēstitūtam corporis vīribus vigōre animī sustinēbat. Dūrāvit hic illī usque ad extrēmum, nec aut spatiō valētūdinis aut metū mortis īnfrāctus est, quō plūrēs graviōrēsque nōbīs causās relinqueret et dēsīderiī et dolōris.

1. **Case Usages.** Locate one phrase in the passage above in which a noun in the dative is used with a compound verb:

   _____

   Locate one phrase in which two nouns in the accusative are used with a compound verb:

   _____

   Locate one phrase in which a noun in the ablative is used with an adjective:

   _____

   Locate three nouns in the ablative expressing means, instrument, or cause:

   _____

   Locate three phrases in the ablative that express manner:

   _____   _____

   _____

2. **Style.** Locate one example of asyndeton:

   _____

   Locate one example of chiastic word order:

   _____

   Locate one example of phrases in which the words are arranged in parallel order:

   _____

   Locate three examples of alliteration:

   _____   _____   _____

Passage 4

Ō trīste plānē acerbumque fūnus! Ō morte ipsā mortis tempus indignius! Iam dēstināta erat ēgregiō iuvenī, iam ēlēctus nūptiārum diēs, iam nōs vocātī. Quod gaudium quō maerōre mūtātum est! Nōn possum exprimere verbīs quantum animō vulnus accēperim, cum audīvī Fundānum ipsum, ut multa lūctuōsa dolor invēnit, praecipientem, quod in vestēs margarīta gemmās fuerat ērogātūrus, hoc in tūs et unguenta et odōrēs impenderētur.

1. **Neuter Nouns.** List, in their nominative and genitive singular forms, seven neuter nouns in the passage above:

   _____

   _____

2. **Present Participle.** Locate one present participle in the passage above: _____
   Write the forms of the full declension of this participle:

   Singular

	Masculine	*Feminine*	*Neuter*
Nom.	_____	_____	_____
Gen.	_____	_____	_____
Dat.	_____	_____	_____
Acc.	_____	_____	_____
Abl.	_____	_____	_____

   Plural

Nom.	_____	_____	_____
Gen.	_____	_____	_____
Dat.	_____	_____	_____
Acc.	_____	_____	_____
Abl.	_____	_____	_____

3. **Future Active Participle.** Locate one future active participle in the passage above:

   _____

4. **Indirect Question.** Locate one indirect question in the passage above:

   _____

   Is this indirect question in primary or secondary sequence? (Circle *primary* or *secondary*.) What would the direct question have been?

   _____

5. *Ut* **with Indicative.** Locate one clause in the passage introduced with *ut* and having its verb in the indicative:

   _____

   When *ut* introduces a clause with its verb in the indicative, *ut* is translated _____

   or _____.

6. **Indirect Command.** Usually indirect commands begin with *ut* or *nē*, but sometimes the conjunction is omitted. Find one example in the passage above of an indirect command that does not begin with a conjunction:

   _____

   What word introduces this indirect command? _____

Passage 5

Est quidem ille ērudītus et sapiēns, ut quī sē ab ineunte aetāte altiōribus studiīs artibusque dēdiderit; sed nunc omnia, quae audiit saepe quae dīxit, aspernātur expulsīsque virtūtibus aliīs pietātis est tōtus. Ignōscēs, laudābis etiam, sī cōgitāveris quid āmīserit.

1. Identification of Verb Forms.

	Mood	*Tense*	*Person*	*Number*
dēderit	_____	_____	_____	_____
audiit	_____	_____	_____	_____
dīxit	_____	_____	_____	_____
aspernātur	_____	_____	_____	_____
ignōscēs	_____	_____	_____	_____
laudābis	_____	_____	_____	_____
āmīserit	_____	_____	_____	_____

2. Ablative Absolute. Locate one ablative absolute in the passage above:

_____

3. Indirect Question. Locate one indirect question in the passage above:

_____

Passage 6

Āmīsit enim fīliam, quae nōn minus mōrēs eius quam ōs vultumque referēbat, tōtumque patrem mīrā similitūdine exscrīpserat. Proinde sī quās ad eum dē dolōre tam iūstō litterās mittēs, mementō adhibēre sōlācium nōn quasi castīgātōrium et nimis forte, sed molle et hūmānum.

1. Fourth Declension Nouns. Locate one 4th declension noun in the passage above:

_____

Decline this noun:

	Singular	*Plural*
Nom.	_____	_____
Gen.	_____	_____
Dat.	_____	_____
Acc.	_____	_____
Abl.	_____	_____

2. Ablative of Manner. Locate one phrase in the ablative that expresses manner:

_____

3. Agreement of Adjectives with Nouns. List the adjectives that modify the following nouns in the passage above:

patrem _____   dolōre _____

similitūdine _____   sōlācium _____

Passage 7

Quod ut facilius admittat, multum faciet mediī temporis spatium. Ut enim crūdum adhūc vulnus medentium manūs reformidat, deinde patitur atque ultrō requīrit, sīc recēns animī dolor cōnsōlātiōnēs rēicit ac refugit, mox dēsīderat et clēmenter admōtīs adquiēscit. Valē.

1. **Adverbs.** Adverbs can modify verbs, adjectives, or other adverbs. In the passage above, what words do the following adverbs modify?

    facilius _____

    adhūc _____

    deinde _____

    ultrō _____

    sīc _____

    mox _____

    clēmenter _____

2. Words or phrases in the genitive case often modify or limit the meaning of nouns on which they depend. What words in the passage above do the following genitives modify?

    mediī temporis _____

    medentium _____

    animī _____

3. **Style.** Roman authors often pair words with one another for rhetorical effect. Locate three pairs of verbs in the passage above:

    _____   _____

    _____   _____

    _____   _____

    In each pair, is the first or the second verb more forceful? (Circle *first* or *second.*)

    How does the final verb bring the letter to an effective conclusion? How does the conclusion of the letter contrast with the beginning (*Trīstissimus haec tibi scrībō. . . .*)?

    _____

    _____

    _____